MW01027837

TIL THE
LAST

SURVIVING THE TRUTH, LIES AND
SECRETS OF THE LAOTIAN CIVIL WAR

CAPTAIN SOUNTHONE RATANAKONE
WITH TODD SAMOVITZ

Elite
PUBLICATIONS

Til The Last: Surviving the Truth, Lies and Secrets of the Laotian Civil War
All Rights Reserved
Copyright © 2022 Til The Last, LLC
First Printing: October 2022

All rights reserved. No portion of this book may be reproduced in any form whatsoever without express written permission from the author.

Every effort has been made by the publisher and the author to ensure that the information contained in this book was correct as of press time. While this publication is designed to provide accurate information in regard to the subject matter covered, the publisher and author assume no responsibility for any errors, inaccuracies, omissions, or any other inconsistencies herein and hereby disclaim any liability to any party for any loss, damage, or disruption caused by error or omissions, regardless of whether any errors or omissions result from negligence, accident, or any other cause.

The stories in this book reflect the author's best recollection of true events, many of which occurred under traumatic and violent circumstances. Some names, locations and identifying characteristics have been changed to protect the safety, confidentiality and privacy of those depicted. Dialogue has been re-created from the author's memory.

For rights and permissions, please contact info@tilthelast.com.

Publisher: Elite Publications
Language: English
Library of Congress Control Number: 9798845865601
Paperback ISBN: 9781958037058
Hardcover ISBN: 9781958037065
eBook ISBN: 9781958037072
Kindle Version Available
Imprint: Independently published
Book Cover and Interior design by: Tiger Shark, Inc.

PRINTED IN THE UNITED STATES OF AMERICA

ACKNOWLEDGEMENTS

I dedicate this book to:

King Sisavang Vatthana, Queen Khamphoui and Crown Prince Vong Savang, all of whom died in the Meoungaviengxai concentration camp in 1978.

My loving grandfather, Praya Nai Ratanakone.

General Khamphan Ratanakone.

General Suradet Ratanakone.

Captain Bounchanh Ratanakone and all the brave man and women of the Kingdom of Laos who lost their lives in communist-run concentration camps.

My adopted father, Sir Dean Murphy, Laotian Knight Commander, who made this book possible.

My lovely wife, Nivanh Sangsida. She has stood by me during all aspects of this process, including translating our numerous interviews and helping me through the stress and emotions of finally telling my story.

My brother-in-law and sister-in-law, Craig and Tana Curit. They heard my story and sensed that I was ready to "tell the world." They helped from the beginning and through every step of the process.

Our writer, Todd Samovitz. Once he joined our team, he has been "all in" and has helped with many aspects of our project.

TABLE OF CONTENTS

"And ye shall know the truth and the truth shall make you free."
-The CIA's unofficial motto, engraved on the wall of the original CIA headquarters building at Langley, Virginia.

When you've heard it, you must see it; when you've seen it, make a judgement with your heart.
-Laotian proverb

FOREWORD

Luckily, while innovation and ideas are sometimes in short supply, they are a renewable source. Captain Sounthone Ratanakone, known today as "Kevin," is one of those who was gifted with a quick and able mind. His incredible story will reveal an insight into his world at a time when many people's world was falling apart. He experienced and endured situations that very few could have survived. In today's world, with all its distractions, most people will only sit down to read one or two books a year. This one is worth reading.

Sir Dean Murphy
Laotian Knights Commander

PREFACE

The United States waged a secret war in Laos between 1960 and 1975. It involved the recruitment and training of a local anti-communist fighting force. It also involved the launching of an awesome bombing campaign. The purpose was to tie down the forces of North Vietnam and their Laotian allies, the Pathet Lao, and to destroy communist supply lines that moved military forces and supplies along the Ho Chi Minh Trail in eastern Laos en route to South Vietnam. It was believed that anti-communist Laotians could win the struggle for their country if they, and not Americans, led the fighting. It was also believed that the U.S. could avoid the colonialism tag if it did not attempt to take over the territory. It was not to be. The secret war in Laos ended in defeat. The U.S. stopped the bombing and then cut off all assistance to its Laotian allies. In 1975, Laos, along with South Vietnam and Cambodia, fell to the communists.

There was an article in *The New York Times* that was published on November 11, 1976. The headline read: "40,000 Reported Held In Harsh Laos Camps." The article reported that "Thousands of former rightist and neutralist Laotians are confined in harsh and repressive internment camps scattered throughout Laos, according to accounts being received here." While the official explanation from the new Lao communist government was that these places were "re-education camps" for "every soldier or civil servants or prominent personality of the foreign government," escaped prisoners told the newspaper reporter a different story. Survivors of the camps said they were forced to "engage in heavy labor, with the food ration about one bowl of rice a day." Anyone "attempting to escape either from the camps or prisons are subject to execution." The death rate was "reportedly high because of the poor diet and lack of medical attention" especially from the "epidemic of malaria and dysentery." The article also noted that the "worst aspect is said to be the psychological, with many people uncertain how long they will have to spend in the camps."

It was not surprising for me to read that there were "only fragmentary newspaper accounts of the camps in Laos" and "virtually nothing about the more repressive camps." What was disappointing for me to read was that "(t)he United States Government has received many of these reports but is reluctant to discuss conditions in the camps publicly for fear that the Laotian authorities may retaliate against the staff of 25 still at the American Embassy in Vientiane, which serves as a listening point on communist activities in Indochina."

I did not learn about this newspaper article until I decided to finally tell my story more than four decades later. The fact is, it would not have been possible for me to read that article in 1976 even if I had wanted to. The reason for that is I was one of those prisoners.

Why did I wait so long to tell my story? The honest answer is I tried hard for the longest time to forget. Even though seconds seemed like hours on the battlefield and in the concentration camp, those memories were painful to hold on to. I could not forget that I had proudly and loyally served the Royal Lao Army, just like my father before me. However, I had witnessed so many unspeakable horrors as a soldier and as a prisoner of war that I just wanted them all to disappear. As I got older, my family grew larger and time seemed to get shorter. I realized life becomes a war between remembering and forgetting.

In the shadows of the Vietnam War, the Central Intelligence Agency (CIA) organized a secret war in Laos to prevent communism from spreading into Southeast Asia. We fought for the U.S., and for ourselves, to keep Ho

Chi Minh's communist regime from destroying our way of life. That objective was not realized. The current communist government in Laos insists that the U.S. lost the wars in Vietnam and Laos, and that is why it pulled out of Southeast Asia. These communists insist that the concentration camps never existed. They deny prisoners were tortured and that they killed members of the Royal Family. These communists have discovered that I was a leader in the Royal Lao Army who killed many of their soldiers during the war, and as an act of revenge, they want to disparage me. These communists must also know that I was a prisoner in their concentration camp. Much of the activities of the Secret War in Laos, including the CIA's involvement in training and arming Lao soldiers, still remain to be declassified or are being lost as the veterans and participants of the war pass away.

For all of these reasons, I realized that I did not want my story, and the story of what happened to my country, to disappear. I wanted to pass on the truth to my children and all future generations. I was reminded how I love my native country of Laos, how I served Laos and the U.S. with all my ability and loyalty, and how I need history to accurately reflect that.

There was a Colonial French saying about their view of the culture of the Lao people: "The Vietnamese plant rice, the Cambodians watch it grow, and the Lao listen to it grow." What is true about my story is also true about the story of my country: if only we had listened better.

INTRODUCTION

In the spring of 1978, I was waiting to die. Deep in the jungle of Laos, I was blindfolded along with six of my fellow concentration camp prisoners. Our Lao communist captors had their guns aimed at us. It was just a matter of when they decided to pull the trigger on me.

I had seen plenty of death up until this moment. I had seen it come quickly. I had also seen death take its own time. That was the worst torment of all – the waiting. As I stood before a firing squad, I felt trembling through my body, but my mind was numb. My life did not flash before my eyes or anything like that. Decades later, after remembering what was one of my many close calls with death, it was clear to me that it was my country's past that brought me to this firing squad. All those years removed from escaping death on that day, the history of my homeland is what now flashed before my eyes.

The history of Laos is full of outside interventions which created internal division within our society. It pains me to admit that, with hindsight, Laotians have taken the wrong approaches for many centuries because political leaders and kings were greedy for power. Political corruption created many internal divisions.

Economic corruption created poverty and social unrest. Social corruption created political divisions. It was vicious circle, one that created an opening for the communists to fill.

I am neither a historian nor a politician. However, a brief history of Laos' long past of political, military, and social conflicts and wars should be outlined to give context to the eventual life or death crossroads I faced when I fought for, and then fled from, my country.

In ancient times, Laos was known as the kingdom of Lan Xang, translated to mean "kingdom of the Million Elephants." The kingdom was served ably by a succession of kings until around the mid-sixteenth century when political power struggles and regional wars resulted in the division of Laos into three governing areas. In the latter half of the 1800s, the French, seeking colonial expansion and economic opportunities, arrived and ultimately conquered Laos. The country was subsequently used as a buffer zone between British interests in Thailand and Burma and French Vietnamese holdings. Eventually, the French were able to reunify the three separated areas of Laos in the early 1900s.

During World War II, the Japanese conquered Laos and evicted the French for a short period of time. After the Japanese surrender in 1945, they assisted separatist movements to officially declare Laotian independent from France. To support this effort, Prince Phetsarath Ratanavongsa of the Lao royal family formed an opposition movement to the reimposition of French control. Prince Phetsarath was helped by his two brothers, Prince Souvanna Phouma and Prince Souphanouvong.

However, the Western powers influenced France's attempt to reclaim Laos. This resulted in increased political opposition and the rise and formation of a resistance movement, the Lao Issara (Free Laos). By September 1946, the French once again controlled and dominated the country, forcing the three brothers into exile and taking with them their governmental philosophies to replace the French. Prince Phetsarath dictated a military clash with the French, Prince Souvanna Phouma wanted to retake Laos with a legitimate political process and Prince Souphanouvong aligned with the communist Viet Minh. Souvanna Phouma eventually won the debate and, through the political process, became the prime minister.

At the time of my birth in 1948, the stage had already been set for the Secret War in Laos because of three ongoing issues: (1) disagreement among the three brothers on which style of government was best for the country, (2) communist expansion, and (3) the United States' manipulation of the differing factions, including sponsoring a proxy war inside the country. When I was much older, I was informed of a cynical quote that described an elephant as "a mouse built to government specifications." As you read my story, you will see how true that is.

CHAPTER ONE

I was born on May 1, 1948 in Luang Prabang, the old capital of Laos. Located in northern Laos, my hometown lies in the valley at the confluence of the Mekong and Nam Khan rivers. Luang Prabang is known for its many Buddhist temples. It was also known as the "King city" because the King's palace was located there, and it served as the royal capital until 1975.

My paternal grandfather was Nai Ratanakone. Grandpa's father was related to the royal family in Japan, and the first part of our last name, "Ratana," is believed to be Japanese. My paternal great grandmother was from Taiwan. My great grandfather was a very successful businessman in Taiwan. My great grandfather's oldest son, Kasen Ratanakone, followed his father into the business world. But my great grandfather wanted his younger son to become a doctor. So that is what Grandpa became. His parents sent him to school in Paris for 12 years. Grandpa not only learned seven different languages, but he became a general doctor, a surgeon and a pharmacist. After earning his licenses, Grandpa worked as a doctor and a surgeon for the French government at the time when Laos was a French colony. He was then sent to Laos, worked with the French Embassy and treated their high ranked officers. At that time, Laos was a small and undeveloped country. Laos did not have a good health care system so the French had to bring their own doctors and medicine. As fortune would have it for Laos, Grandpa was very good at his profession. Grandpa's older brother, Kasen, also went to Laos for a short while but then he eventually moved to Thailand. Like his father, Kasen did very well in business. The last name of Ratanakone became associated with many successful businesspeople in Thailand.

After Grandpa moved to Laos and began practicing medicine, he assisted one of the French generals in the small village of Mouang Gnoy. Mouang Gnoy was located near the city of Nambak which was a province in Luang Prabang. While Grandpa was helping the General, he was asked to treat another man who was sick. It was during that time that Grandpa met that man's daughter, a beautiful young lady named Kanchan. Grandpa fell in love with Kanchan, married her and ended up staying in Luang Prabang for the rest of his life.

Grandpa became very successful and beloved in his new hometown. He treated the French military officers and government workers. He delivered babies, set broken bones, and served as a licensed pharmacist. Grandpa also became the personal doctor to Sisavang Vong, the King of Laos, as well as to the entire Royal Family. Grandpa became so close to the Royal Family that the palace would send out a chauffeur to pick up Grandpa during the weekend to play bridge with the King. Grandpa was soon able to afford a big house with a separate house in the back. He used that separate area as his medical office, pharmacy and a small hospital that could house up to 36 patients. Grandpa performed small surgeries at home and performed more complicated surgeries at the larger Mahosod Hospital. Grandpa also took care of those who did not have any money to pay for his services. When someone asked Grandpa how much their care was going to cost, he would say, "Get better first, and then pay what you can. If you can't pay, then don't worry." Grandpa treated everyone, and he did not want their finances to affect their treatment. In turn, Grandpa's patients did not take advantage of his generosity. Without fail, his patients would eventually pay him something, be it cash, jewelry or pigs and chickens.

     Grandpa's success and kindness afforded him the ability to take care of children from families who could not afford to raise them. He always welcomed abandoned children and orphans into his home. He even adopted some of them and gave them his own last name. One of these children he adopted was a baby named Ouane. My Uncle Ouane would grow up to be a polarizing figure in our family and our country.

In recognition for the good Grandpa did for the community, King Sisavang Vong, honored him by granting him the first name "Phaya." Phaya is the equivalent of "Lord" or "Sir" in England. The King only gave this name to those who served their country either by honorable civil service or military service. It is the highest title one can have, and not many people in Laos earn that honor. The King continued to honor Grandpa's family by having one of Grandpa's sons, who became a goldsmith and jeweler, to make the crown and other items for him and his queen.

Like Grandpa, my maternal grandparents also came from royal lines. My maternal grandfather, Chao Oune Vongkot, could trace his royal line back to Chao Anouvong, one of the famous kings in Laos. My maternal grandmother, Chao Panekham Ounkham, was the daughter of Oun Kham, the king of Luang Prabang. King Oun Kham served two reigns, the first one from 1872 to 1887, and a second one between 1889 and 1895. His reigns

4

were interrupted because on June 7, 1887 Laos' royal capital was seized and sacked. The elderly king barely escaped with his life, and he was exiled to Bangkok. It was there that the King assisted Auguste Jean-Marie Pavie. Pavie was a French colonial civile servant who was instrumental in establishing French control over Laos. As a result of this partnership, the last two years of King Oun Kham's reign ended with the establishment of a French protectorate over Laos.

Like the many royal generations before them, the marriage of my parents, Khamphane Ratanakone and Chao Khanchanh Ounkham, had been arranged. My father was born in Luang Prabang province, the old capital of Laos, in July of 1920. When he met my mother, my father was an officer and tank commander in the Royal Lao Army. My father chose a military career because Grandpa wanted his sons to fight for their country's freedom. Grandpa was close to the French generals, and he heard a lot about the political storm that was brewing in Laos. That storm was the threat of communism. Grandpa had heard enough to convince him that the communists were not going to make people's lives better and he instilled that belief into his sons.

My father and his younger brother were in the very first class at the first military school in Laos which was called Dong Hen. Located on a military base in Savannaket province, Dong Hen was run by the French because Laos was still a French colony. My father was very smart, one of the top students in his class, as was my uncle. They both attended the school for two and a half years, then they were assigned to Paris for more military training for three more years.

My father was married once before he met my mother. His first wife was not from a royal family, and she was an elementary school teacher. My father had three children with his first wife; two boys and one girl. The marriage ended because while my father was away on military duty, his first wife committed adultery. When my father returned home, he discovered the crime of his wife and divorced her.

My mother truly came from what would be known as a "palace family." It was very similar to Chinese culture, where males were considered more prestigious and kings had more than one wife. The more wives a king had, the more power he had. In my mother's family, the front palace housed the King's first wife and the higher royals. The back palace was for the servant wives. My mother lived in the front palace, and she was the youngest of four, and the only girl.

When my father met my mother, my father was already "pre-approved" by my mother's family; they recognized Grandpa's royal lines from Japan and Taiwan. They also recognized that Grandpa was not only a good and well-connected man but he was also well off. He owned houses and places of business for the entire family and their in-laws.

My father and mother had seven children, and I was the oldest. Being a high-ranking soldier, my father was away from home much of the time, either on military bases or fighting on the front lines. Most of the time, my mother would follow my father to the military bases to live with him. Growing up, I would only see my father every three or four months, and he would stay home for only four or five days. My siblings and I always looked forward to our father returning home. He would pile us into a military jeep, drive around town and then take us to the movies. After the movies, he would take us to the scenic Khan riverbank and buy us food from a local vendor. In Luang Prabang, the Khan River passed through the city. On the coconut tree-lined riverbanks, people enjoyed strolling around or relaxing by the water and watching the boats go by. Local vendors would station their pushcarts under the coconut trees and set up seats for customers near the carts. My favorite vendor food was pho which was a beef or chicken broth with rice noodles and vegetables. I also enjoyed a Vietnamese dish which was made with meat and flat noodles rolled up and topped with sweet chili sweet and sour sauce. The vendors served each dish in banana leaf bowls. I also really liked the blended icy fruit drink, coconut ice cream and wild black rice ice cream. This is what our father did with us every time he came home, and it was a fun and memorable routine.

Since my father was away so much, I became very close to Grandpa, and we would spend a lot of time together. It was clear that out of his 22 grandchildren, I was the favorite one. I was the only grandchild who would help Grandpa at work. I would sterilize needles and surgical instruments by boiling them before he treated patients. I would also retrieve his medicine from his storage room and learned which ones treated which conditions. I was also the only grandchild who was allowed to accompany Grandpa to the King's palace to play bridge during the weekend. I got to drive in the King's chauffeured car with Grandpa and the King's sister.

While Grandpa played bridge, I played with the 20 or so princes and princesses that lived in the palace. At first, I was nervous to join them until they invited me to play with them. Most importantly, I learned some valuable lessons during my time with Grandpa. For example, Grandpa would tell me, "You need to treat people like I do, with respect. You see I treat the young, old, poor and rich the same. You do the same and you will be good." Grandpa would mention to people that he wanted me to become a doctor like him. When Grandpa's patients came in groups to pay him with gold or silver bars, it would be my job to put the bars in bags, drag the bags to the stairwell in Grandpa's house and then hide them under the stairs. As payment for me helping him, Grandpa would pay me with French chocolate bars. Even though none of my cousins helped Grandpa, they wanted me to share the chocolate with them. At the end of his long day at work, I would massage Grandpa to help him sleep.

I remember when Grandpa's family from Japan and Taiwan came to visit Laos. Grandpa spoke Japanese, and when he introduced me to the Japanese royal family, Grandpa said, "This grandson of mine is a really intelligent boy and I want him to be a doctor like me." Grandpa's family traveled with their own servants and drove fancy cars. The ladies wore kimonos and the men dressed very well. I noticed the family only spoke to Grandpa. Like our family from Japan and Taiwan, we grew up in comfortable surroundings in Luang Prabang. Grandpa had a lot of land, property, housekeepers, and cooks.

I began my formal education in 1953 at an elementary school called TA Frank which was a Catholic school for upper class parents to send their kids to. To be closer to my father's military base, we moved to the new capital of Vientiane which was close to the Mekong River and across from Thailand. Since my mother lived on the military base with my father, my siblings and I lived with an aunt who was my father's sister. She and her husband had two large houses, and my siblings and I lived with our cousins in one of them. My father provided two Mercedes vans that drove us to school and wherever else we needed to go. We were also assigned security guards from the military to protect us. My father was a high-ranking officer, helping the French fight against the Chinese and North Vietnamese Army so not all was peaceful and safe on the home front. Consequently, my father always had to always have troops around him and his family.

Many of my cousins in Vientiane were older than me and my siblings. When meals were served, it was usually first come, first serve and the older cousins would muscle in and get the food first. This would upset me, especially if there wasn't much food left, and I would cry. My aunt and uncle did not care much about this situation, even though my father was sending money to them to keep up the extra household expenses.

Sometimes my older half-brother Thao Yai, one of the sons from my father's first marriage, would come to stay with my aunt and cousins. He would often be mean to me and beat me up. I would tell Thao Yai, "Wait until I grow bigger, I will fight you back."

This aunt I was staying with caused problems for our family. One problem was that my aunt did not like my mother. During my father and mother's visits, my aunt would bully my mother because of her kindness. When my mother went to the market, she would buy extra things and she would share with people who were less fortunate. When poor people in Laos and Thailand would ask for help with food and clothing, my mother would always answer their call. There was a caste system in Asia in general, and in Laos in particular; royals and upper class did not associate with the lower class. My aunt was well educated and well connected. She owned the bank in Vientiane and she associated with all of the wealthy and powerful people. Even though my mother came from a royal family, she was not as socialized like my aunt. To make matters worse for my mother, my aunt preferred my father's first wife. She thought the first wife was classier than my mother, even though she was just a teacher. My aunt thought of my mother as a plain country girl.

Another problem was that I was also looked down on, and not treated well, by my aunt because she thought of me as the son of a country girl. Simply put, this aunt was a snob. However, neither my mother nor I ever reacted or responded to this aunt's behavior towards us. My father was a different story. While my father was away on military duty, a local villager wanted to give a baby cow to him. My aunt did not want to take care of the baby cow while my father was away. I took care of that cow so she would not get rid of it. She also did not want to take care of me. When my aunt knew that my father was coming home, my aunt did not let me take care of the cow so she could make it look like she was doing it. My aunt would also dress me up nice to make it appear that I was being taken care of by her. On a few occasions, when my father came home, I told him the truth about how I was being treated. My father asked my aunt about how she was treating me. She said I talked too much, that I was lying, and I did not know any better. She promised my father that she treated all the children in the family equally. I also complained about my aunt to my mother. My mother, who had a more passive and quiet personality, did not want to create any problems. She simply told me to be patient with my aunt and "to do my best."

With all due respect to my dear mother, I ran out of patience with my aunt. I suggested to my father that the next time he decided to come home, to make the visit unannounced so he could check in on me without my aunt knowing. On the day the surprise visit happened, my father asked a house staff member where I was. He was told that I was in the field taking care of the cow. Sure enough, my father found me under a tree doing homework and taking care of the cow. My father was very mad at his sister, and he took me and my siblings out from her house. My father would have preferred for my aunt and her family to move out but they had nowhere else to go. My father ended up moving us into our own house.

We now lived near the Mekong River, and that was where I learned how to swim. My friends already knew how to swim so they were the ones who taught me. When they took me out to the river, I just jumped in, and my friends had to save me each time. Eventually, I got better at staying above water by paddling. When I was 10, the tide was very high and rough in the Mekong. We would jump from the tamarind trees with big branches into the raging water. I had no choice but to become a strong swimmer in these waters. It was a developed skill that, unbeknownst to me at the time, would serve me well later in life.

Looking back on stories like these, I believe I was fortunate to have inherited the best qualities from my parents. My father was brave, honest, a fighter and did not like to talk much unless he had to. He would often tell me and my siblings, "You need to be a good person, love the country when you grew up in and be good to your mother and listen to her." My mother was a very patient, kind and genuine person. When I was a boy, I would follow her example and I would help out poor people who needed rice and clothing. If my parents were not home, I would ask the housekeepers to give the poor a lot of rice. I would also sneak into my mother's closet, take her fine silk dresses and give them away. I thought she would never miss them because she had so many!

CHAPTER TWO

During my early years growing up, I was unaware of the important political and military changes going on in Laos. These changes are worth briefly outlining because they would directly and significantly impact my future.

In 1950, the French established Vietnam, Laos, and Cambodia as associated states within the French Union. As the communist threat grew within this Union, the U.S. began military aid to the French to help stop its spread. By 1952, the United States was paying for a portion of the French war costs.

Frustrated at the continuing presence of the French in Laos, Prince Souphanouvong convened a revolutionary congress and formed a resistance government. The new congress formed for war and established its political arm, the Lao Patriotic Front, and an action arm, later to be named the Pathet Lao.

The Pathet Lao communist resistance front formed with the assistance of the Viet Minh to defeat the French and Royal Laotian Government's (RLG) allies. It was headed by the Resistance Committee of Eastern Laos with Prince Souphanouvong accepted as its nominal leader. The first guerrilla force was formed in January 1949. The recruits for this fighting unit were from the hill tribes, including the Tai and Hmong.

In 1950, over 150 members of the movement met with Ho Chi Minh, and the organization renamed itself the Neo Lao Issara (Free Lao Front) with its armed wing incorporating the Pathet Lao. They adopted a Maoist people's revolutionary war strategy and began their guerrilla warfare phase. The Viet Minh conventional forces from North Vietnam as well as China and Russia militarily supplied and supported the Pathet Lao.

In response, the French deployed one colonial battalion per province. With French training to raise a Lao military force, the first two 600-man battalions of the RLG were formed. In 1951, with the addition of two infantry battalions and one parachute battalion, Laos' total military manpower reached about 5,000. Owing to U.S. military aid, the number of battalions increased and were provided with American arms and equipment. Additional counterinsurgency units were formed to expand the capabilities and number of government security forces.

In 1953, four infantry divisions of the Viet Minh, along with 2,000 Pathet Lao forces led by Prince

Souphanouvong, tried to capture Luang Prabang. They were also successful in capturing the province of Sam Neua where they immediately established a rebel government. To assist in the fight to recapture this vital area, the CIA Civil Air Transport (CAT) subsidiary asset assisted the French from May to June 1953 with C-119 paradrops. CAT was later to become "Air America."

In 1954, the Viet Minh defeated French forces at the Battle of Dien Bien Phu and the whole security dynamic in the region changed. The Geneva Conference of May 1954 split Vietnam into North and South, while Laos was declared independent and neutral. A ceasefire was implemented in Laos in August 1954 to remove foreign troops and to demobilize and integrate Pathet Lao forces into the government's military forces. The Geneva Conference and Agreement of 1954 spelled out the new security arrangement for Laos. Two of the key provisions were as follows: (1) Prohibiting introduction into Laos of foreign or regular troops, or irregular troops, foreign paramilitaries, or foreign military personnel and (2) Prohibiting introduction into Laos of armaments, munitions, and war material, except for conventional items necessary for the RLG to defend itself.

In response, U.S. policy objectives were to (1) maintain a pro-U.S. country (or at least a neutral government in Laos), (2) secure freedom from communism, (3) disrupt the flow of communist supplies, and (4) adhere to the spirit of the Geneva Accords. The U.S. strategy consisted of a political warfare covert operation, using clandestine interagency assets and unconventional warfare with special operations forces as needed, combined with the conduct of foreign internal defense and security assistance programs. President Dwight D. Eisenhower also acted to counteract subversive communist activities still ongoing throughout the region with increased aid to Thailand and South Vietnam. The diplomatic response to the threat created a new security organization, the Southeast Asia Treaty Organization (SEATO). With the many restrictions of the Geneva Convention, the priority of effort was focused on Thailand as a defensive measure against aggression, starting with foreign aid programs, followed by military aid programs. The U.S. military then established the Military Advisory Assistance Group (MAAG) with a buildup of military bases in Thailand to support the U.S. Air Force and combat advisors' operations.

The Geneva Accords of 1954 marked the end of French rule in Southeast Asia. It left the Kingdom of Laos a very fragile country because there were conflicting factions. The Vientiane government, headed by Prime Minister Souvanna Phouma, was an uneasy coalition of neutralists, led by the prime minister, and communist-oriented Pathet Lao with Souvanna's half-brother, Prince Souphanouvong, serving as its "nominal" military and political leader. There were separate military groupings with the neutralists controlling the Royal Lao Army and a Pathet Lao army occupying two northern provinces, Houa Phan, also called Samneua, and Phong Saly. The population of three million included a small, French-educated elite and numerous diverse, uneducated tribal groups who lived in isolated jungle and mountainous areas.

The U.S. supported, but did not sign, the 1954 Geneva agreements. It believed that the free world's interest required keeping Laos and two other newly created Indochina states, South Vietnam, and Cambodia, out of the grips of communist North Vietnam, China, and the Soviet Union. The provisions regarding Laos forbade the Vientiane government from entering into any foreign military alliance, called for the withdrawal of all foreign troops except a French military training mission, and limited the types and amount of military equipment that could be used by the small Royal Lao Army of 10,000 men. Also established was an International Control Commission (ICC) to ensure compliance with the provisions.

Given Laos' weaknesses, the problematic Geneva terms and the U.S.' suspicions of the communist nations of Hanoi, Peking, and Moscow, enforcing Laos' neutrality was difficult. The Pathet Lao prevented the ICC from entering its occupied area, and Hanoi continued to train, equip, and support the Pathet Lao.

Between 1955 and 1958, over $200 million dollars in U.S. aid had been funneled to Laos. This money resulted in widespread corruption within the Lao government. Throughout the 1950's and early 1960's, the U.S. did its best to support a neutral Laos in a volatile political and military environment. Despite U.S. efforts, the Lao government was threatened not only by the Pathet Lao but by a rightist faction. Souvanna Phouma resigned as prime minister on July 23, 1958, and Prince Tiao Somsanith became prime minister. Somsanith was then overthrown and Souvanna Phouma was once again named prime minister. After Souvanna was reinstated, fighting broke out among the various factions, and the communist nations became very interested in taking over Laos. The Soviet Union, for example, not only supported the Pathet Lao but also started to support the North Vietnamese Army (NVA).

Tensions and conflicts were such that our King and Prime Minister traveled to the United States to ask for its help. As a result, a Declaration on the Neutrality of Laos was agreed to on July 23, 1962. Fourteen nations agreed to reaffirm the 1954 Geneva agreement by declaring a neutral Laos, the withdrawal of foreign troops, and supervision of the agreement by the ICC.

Unfortunately, the mutual suspicions between the U.S. and its communist adversaries over each other's activities in Laos did not disappear. Washington continued to assist General Vang Pao's guerilla army, now between 14,000 and 18,000 men. Hanoi, with China's support, refused to withdraw most of its troops from Laos. Each side accused each other of not abiding by the Declaration of Neutrality. The United States and the communists now stepped-up sending supplies to their respective allies. The battles were surely going to lead to war.

During these political and military changes and challenges, my father worked for the U.S. government to fight against the communists. While there were not many political discussions during my childhood, my father made it a point to tell us that the communists were liars. "They say one thing and do another," he would always say. I remember my father telling me about when he caught communist soldiers and interrogated them. He would ask them, "Why did you become a communist? Why are you fighting us? Why do you want to kill us? Why do you want to kill Americans?" One of my father's prisoners, a young communist soldier, admitted that he had grown up learning to hate Americans. He said that many communist soldiers were orphans who were raised in government homes. They were told that their parents were killed by Americans. It was obvious that the young generation was being brainwashed. The older communist soldiers had a much different response. When my father asked those captured soldiers the same question, they said if they did not listen to the communists and do what they said, their families back home would be killed. My father did not know about the politics of communism until he was fighting them; he certainly did not learn about it during his schooling. For these reasons, my father tried to educate us quickly about the threat of communism.

CHAPTER THREE

When I began my formal academic education, things went quickly. I skipped some grades, from kindergarten to third grade to sixth grade and then to ninth grade. Every time the school would give me an aptitude test, I would pass it and they would skip me. The same thing happened to my younger brother, Phonesavath. While it may have made my parents proud, being with kids who were much older than me in the classroom was a problem. I certainly got bullied. Fortunately, I was taught to fight starting at age seven. My instructor was one of my father's main staff soldiers who also happened to be one of our family security guards. Sergeant Khamphet Thommasane was a professional Thai boxer, and he also had a black belt in Kung Fu. He was a big man and he stood about 6'2" tall. When I was about five or six years old, I would watch Sergeant Thommasane train. I asked him a lot of questions about what he was doing, and I told him that I wanted to learn how to fight like him. Sergeant Thommasane told me I was too young to learn how to fight. When I was seven, he finally agreed to teach me how to fight because I was his general's son. However, he told me that if I did not like the training, he would stop teaching me. There was not a possibility in my mind that I would not like it. I wanted to learn everything Sergeant Thommasane knew.

I quickly learned that Sergeant Thommasane was very much like me. We were both quiet and serious, so we ended up getting along very well. As tough as he was, Sergeant Thommasane also only allowed his mother to cut his hair. She lived two or three hours away in southern Laos, but the military allowed him to fly there to have his mother cut his hair. This custom was based on a religious belief that only a true protector could cut his hair.

Sergeant Thommasane's training was very intense. He had me do push-ups on my fingers. I ran many miles. I punched a bag until my fists were raw. I stood on my head for a long time to build up my neck muscles. He taught me how to use nunchucks, fighting sticks, throwing knives and swords. He taught me that all weapons were extensions of my hands so even if the weapons were taken from me, I could continue to defend myself. Sergeant Thommasane emphasized to me that as important as it was to be in control of my fighting movements, I had to keep an eye out for the movements made by my opponent. He taught me the weak spots in the human body to attack, like the side of the neck, under the armpit, under the heart and inside of the leg. Those body parts were very vulnerable because major arteries were located under them.

Even though I was his commanding officer's son, Sergeant Thommasane never took it easy on me. He had me to stand in the bottom of a hole he constructed and then he made me jump up a step at a time with weights tied to my legs. When I removed the weights from my legs, I remember feeling very light but very strong. We also did sparring sessions. During these sessions, the movements started out very slowly then we sped up the sparring movements over time to mimic a real fight. I got hit and kicked every day which toughened me up very quickly. I also quickly became an expert in hand-to-hand combat, and how to attack a person's weakest and vulnerable spots. Sergeant Thommasane also taught me to shoot a gun as part of our training. It was one of my favorite things to learn and it was a skill that would come in handy later in my life. Sergeant Thommasane was my teacher for almost 10 years. His discipline always amazed me. He lived almost a hermit's existence and lived strictly by the Five Precepts that, at the time, seemed to me impossible to live by.

Inevitably, I put Sergeant Thommasane's teachings into practice. When I was 12 years old, I was seated at the front of the class because, as usual, I was smaller and younger than everybody else. An older boy who had repeatedly failed the class, kept knocking on my head with his knuckle. He was not hitting me softly. This older boy may not have been smart enough to get promoted to the next grade, but he was smart enough to wait until the teacher wrote on the board with her back to us before he hit me. I kept asking the older boy to stop, but he kept knocking on my head. I finally said, "If you don't stop, I'm going to tell the sister-teacher." "Sister-teacher" was what all female teachers were called at the time. My threat did nothing to stop the older boy from hitting me. I then told the teacher what this boy was doing. I could not believe it, but the teacher ignored my complaint. The next time the older boy knocked my head with his knuckle, I could not take it anymore. I jumped on the table, and I kicked the older boy as hard as I could. I was so mad that I cannot recall to this day where I kicked him exactly, but it was somewhere between his chin and his neck. This got the teacher's attention, finally. Even though my classmates were witnesses and told the teacher I was being bullied by the older boy, we both ended up getting into trouble. We had to stand in front of the class and hold our hands out while the teacher hit our hands with a stick.

I thought this bad day at school was over, but I was wrong. This older boy threatened to beat me up after school for what I did to him. I remembered what Sergeant Thommasane had taught me. He said if I was going to fight a boy bigger than me, I would have to start the fight first and end it first. The older boy and I agreed to meet at a certain place to fight. As soon as I got out of school that day, I ran off and hid in a ditch near the canal where we were going to fight. I waited for the older boy to come looking for me. When he finally arrived, I ambushed him and beat him up until he was black and blue. The older boy fell into a nearby canal and he cried, "Why did you beat me up?!" I told him, "You said you were going to beat me up after school, so I had to get to you first!" The older boy's mom took him to see my parents and demanded damages because I beat their son up. My father asked me why I did it, so I explained what happened. My father still agreed to pay the family and he made me apologize to the boy.

Coming from a general's well-off family had its disadvantages. Most of the kids of higher-ranking families did not need to or want to work; they would rather sit at home and play. But even at a young age, I was driven to work and learn. During one of my three-month summer breaks from school, I wanted to get some work experience. I was looking for a job when I saw a "Help Wanted" sign looking for laborers. I knew that because of my father status as a general and my family's prominent last name it would be hard to get a job as a laborer. People did not want to order a general's son to do work and they did not want to be responsible if I got injured. Also, if the wages were small, they would feel pressure to pay me more than other kids on the job. Almost everyone knew everyone in Vientiane, so getting and keeping this job was going to be tricky.

I went to the place that was looking for laborers. It was a Japanese construction company that wanted to turn a big lake into a shopping center. When I applied for the job, I gave them a fake name and fake family history on the application. I also added that I came from a poor family, and that I needed a job to help support the family. I finally added that I was looking for any labor job they would offer me. The company assumed I was a smart kid and they offered me the job to help clean out the lake. I was given a shovel and long rubber shoes and was told to get started.

My job was to clear the garbage and branches out of the lake. There were countless sticks and thorns in the water. There was no escaping getting scratched all over my body and face. I made the mistake of mentioning to the boss that the thorns were hurting me. The boss yelled at me to get back out there and do my job. I explained to him how the lake was not safe, and I did not want to risk getting more seriously injured. The boss reminded me that <u>he</u> was the boss and not to talk back to him. He then demanded to know who I was. I said that I was just a boy from a poor family, that I needed the money and that I would do the job. The boss said, "OK, I will give you more time, but you need to finish your job." Maybe he felt badly for yelling at me because he then asked me if he had eaten lunch yet. When I said, "No," the boss offered me a lunch box filled with Japanese food. I remember liking that lunch very much.

It took me two weeks to clean out the lake. On one of the last days, when I was ready to finish for the day and get paid, the worst possible thing happened: my mother and her military security guard/chauffer drove to the job site in a military jeep. Someone must have told her that I was working there. When the boss saw the military jeep, he rushed over and demanded to know what my mother and the chauffer were doing here. My mother shot back at the boss, "What is my son doing here? He is the son of a general!" She was afraid of what others would think of my father, specifically that he was not taking care of his family. Startled by this news, the boss explained that he was told by me that I was a poor boy. He also said that I was a good worker, and it would be an honor for me to keep working for him. Noticing my mother's look and silence, the boss added that normal pay for the job was 8,000 kip but because I was the son of the general, he would pay me 19,100 kip. "After all," the boss nervously sputtered, "I do not want to shame the general and his family." Of course, I did not think like that; I just wanted to work and learn. My father found out about this incident and wanted me to explain what happened. I told him that I wanted to have a job, to be able to work hard and do a good job and wanted to know what other people do. I was not thinking about what "class" I was from. My father understood but he was also worried the people would look down at him and ask, "Why would you allow your son to do that?" This was the clear-cut way the class system at the time in Laos. However, I think my father also admired what I was trying to do. He allowed me to finish out the job during the summer. I also was promoted to the foreman position even though I was only 14 years old.

I always just wanted to see how people worked different jobs so I could learn how to do things. One time I sneaked out of the house to help a friend's family who were laborers. My friend's father had some workers who did not show up that day and he needed help. I helped them fix some things in a house. My friend's father offered to pay me, but I refused the money. I just wanted to learn how to fix the problems in the house.

Another job that I had was working for a local Chinese businessman. This man lived in the same neighborhood as me. He owned a coffee shop and sold food. He also owned a bus to transport kids to and from school. The businessman needed to hire a "busboy" who monitored the kids' behavior on the bus. I asked for the job. The businessman said that he could not offer me a job because of who my father was. He knew my father because, when my father came home from the military base, he was a customer of the businessman's store. I simply asked the businessman to not tell my father about it. That did the trick and I worked for the businessman for two and a half months. One day my cousin found out where I was working, and he told my father. Once again, I had to remind my father that I just wanted to learn and to work and to be independent. Once again, my mother did not want me to work as a laborer. Once again, I was reminded that the higher one was in Lao society the more difficult it was to find a 'regular job' as people looked down at the family's reputation. I was also reminded that Grandpa taught me to treat everyone equally. Taking that lesson to heart, I did not look at honest hard work as being beneath me. It would be a lesson that would always serve me well later in life.

As I completed my secondary education, my father made it known that he wanted me to follow his career path and join the military. He was strong in his belief that if there was not a strong military in Laos, we would lose our country to the communists. He put his life on the line because of this belief. For example, in 1960, there was a battle in Savannakhet province when the NVA entered Laos. The enemy burned down a lot of houses and buildings in that area. Between the Royal Lao forces and the communist forces, close to 20,000 men were fighting. My father was a tank commander, and he was wounded in that battle; he was shot in the neck and his right leg. One of my uncles, my father's younger brother, also fought in that battle and he got shot in his left arm. They were lucky to be alive after that battle.

A few years later in the hotter than usual summer of 1964, another battle broke out against the Lao Communists in Xiengkhouang province. My father, his son Bounchanh Ratanakone, and my father's younger brother, Suradet Ratanakone, all fought in this battle. Bounchanh was 12 years older than me and was one of the two sons from my father's first marriage. Bounchanh and I were very much alike personality-wise, and we got along well. He was very much the opposite of my other half-brother Thao Yai. While Bounchanh was completing his military training, he would sometimes come by to visit the family during his breaks. When Bounchanh came to visit he would bring gifts for me and my younger siblings, like food, clothing, toys, and shoes. He would also take us to the market and would treat us to whatever we wanted. Bounchanh would tell me that I needed to be a good person, do well in school and do not get involved in anything that will destroy your life. He was a good brother. My uncle was also a good person. He was down to earth and humble. He really loved his family. He was also very handsome. Once, he took his troops into a village in a very dangerous military zone. The village mayor's daughter really liked my uncle. My uncle looked young for his age so he did not appear like he would be married with a family. When my uncle was asked if he was married, my uncle replied that he was, but no one believed him. The mayor took his daughter to Vientiane to find my uncle's wife and family to confirm that my uncle was telling the truth! Times have changed but back then, arranged marriages were the custom. Families wanted nothing more than their daughters to marry the most suitable and successful men in their respective social class.

My uncle and half-brother, like my father, were tank commanders. During the battle in Xiengkhouang province, the Royal Lao Army was severely outnumbered by 30,000 NVA and Chinese communist troops. The good news was that the communist troops were more concerned with quantity than quality of fighters, and they were generally afraid of the Lao soldiers. The enemy launched an all-out assault, bombarding the terrain without pause. My father had to retreat, and he was separated from my uncle and my half-brother's troops. My father took a position near one mountain, and my uncle took a position near another mountain. My half-brother was in the same area as our uncle, although he was in a different tank.

The communists surrounded my uncle's tank. My uncle kept shooting at them until he ran out of ammunition. The communists then attempted to swarm his tank, but my uncle would run over them. He drove his tank until he ran out of fuel. My uncle was badly outnumbered by the communists. They covered my uncle's tank window with mud. They then attacked his tank with their B41 machine guns. The bullets pierced the tank's armor and created two holes into the tank. The communists then threw a hand grenade into the tank. The explosion hurt my uncle enough where he could not escape from the tank. First, the communists took shots at my uncle while he was inside the tank. Somehow the bullets missed him. But then the communists dragged my uncle out of the tank, beat him up, and then stabbed him until he died. The communists threw my uncle's body back into the tank, threw more grenades inside and blew up it up. My half-brother's tank was also attacked nearby, and he met the same horrible fate as my uncle. The communists left the two tanks there in the battlefield and they took control over the area.

While his forces were defeated, my father walked away unharmed from his battle site. He walked for nine days with 85 of his surviving soldiers. A helicopter picked them up and took him and his troops to Vangvieng. My father did not learn about the death of his brother and son until he returned to Vientiane. I recall my father getting the news while I was home from school on summer break. Even though my father was devastated, he interviewed men from his brother's team who had seen both Suradet and Bounchanh get killed by the NVA.

My father wasted no time asking permission to go back to the battlefield in Xiengkhouang to win back the area. In fact, every man who fought at Xiengkhouang volunteered to go back. This time, my father and his troops avenged their loss and beat the communists. After the victory, despite the dead bodies all over the place, my father found the remains of his son. Unfortunately, he could not find the remains of his brother. My father brought Bounchanh's body back to Vientiane. The King and Prime Minister attended Bounchanh's private funeral at the family house as well as the public funeral at the military base. As a tribute to my Uncle Suradet, Bounchanh, and all the Royal Lao military heroes who gave their lives at Xiengkhouang, those two tanks are still on the battlefield to this day.

CHAPTER FOUR

As the military and political situation in Laos intensified, I continued my education. In addition to my high school classes, I took college level classes as well. I was 16 years old when I graduated high school. I decided that I wanted to be a military judge so I applied to law school. One of the reasons I wanted to go to law school was because of my Uncle Ouane.

At that time, Uncle Ouane was a major-general in the Royal Lao Army. He was a menacing looking man with a broad full face, thick lips and closely cropped hair. He was one of the children who Grandpa adopted. Even though Uncle Ouane knew he was not blood related, he was treated equally and never had any problem with the family. Unfortunately, Uncle Ouane was involved in a business that proved to be problematic to our family. He was rumored to be the kingpin of Laos' opium trade. In fact, Uncle Ouane had boasted to a delegation in Nam Keung, a border area in northwestern Laos which served as a smuggling route for opium, that he had acted as the official controller of the opium trade since 1962. Uncle Ouane transported the opium via military airplanes to a U.S. military base in Thailand. The opium would then be manufactured into heroin. Uncle Ouane was very rich, and he owned a big mansion. In the large basement of that mansion was where his opium factory was. Some attempts were made to raid Uncle Ouane's operations and stop his business, but those people got paid off with a lot of money.

During family discussions, Grandpa told Uncle Ouane that he was one of the sons in the family. Grandpa said his children and grandchildren do not do illegal things, and he expected Uncle Ouane to keep his last name clear and clean. Grandpa said, "I am helping people so no one from my family should do harm to anybody." Grandpa finally said to Uncle Ouane, "I know what you do, you carry my last name, I raised you since you were a little baby so do not destroy my last name. Even though you are not my bloodline, I raised you since you were a little baby." Uncle Ouane tapped Grandpa's shoulder and boasted, "Do you know who I am? Nobody can defeat me. I am second from the Prime Minister." Grandpa did not back down from Uncle Ouane and told him, "You have money? I have more than you. You have houses? I have more than you. You have land? I have more than you." After Grandpa left the meeting, my father said to Uncle Ouane, "You should not be saying that in front of our father. You know how upset he will be. He wants you to be good. He doesn't want his good name and reputation harmed." Uncle Ouane was too proud of himself to watch his tongue. Later, when my father was not around, Uncle Ouane warned all of the grandchildren, "If you became police or go in the military, you don't dare to arrest me or I will cut off your neck." It upset me when I heard what Uncle Ouane said so I went to see Grandpa. Grandpa was very upset by what Uncle Ouane had said. I gave Grandpa a massage to calm him down and told him, "Don't worry, Grandpa. When I grow up, I will arrest him." Grandpa said, "If you can, I would be so happy. I will pray for you." Grandpa then warned Uncle Ouane never to talk to the grandchildren like that again. Uncle Ouane agreed. He ended up changing his last name so he could continue his opium business and to avoid being associated with Grandpa.

From an early age, I wanted to make sure the legal system could be used to stop people like Uncle Ouane from doing bad things. During my last year in high school, I spoke to Grandpa and my father about my decision. Both of them were supportive and told me what next steps I needed to take. I took the entrance exam for the one law school in the province called Vientiane Law

School of Laos. I did very well on the exam and gained admission to the law school. The first-year class had 65 students and, once again, everyone was older and taller than me. The other students were jealous of me because I was so young. They also thought I only was accepted into law school because of who my family was. They did not go out of their way to include me in any of their groups. The professors, to their credit, sensed what was going on. They would ask me questions in class to show the other students that I could hold my own and that me being admitted had nothing to do with my family connections. They were trying to help me be accepted by my classmates. Once the other students learned who I really was as a person, they were more willing to accept me. They would soon come to me to ask questions about the material, and I would help them out. I was also included in their groups.

Law school was a four-year program. Like most law schools around the world, professors used the Socratic method to teach us. Like most law school professors, they were also very strict and demanding. I had to remember a lot of laws and had to know right away what laws applied to which situations. During this time in 1965, my grandfather Phaya Nai Ratanakone died at the age of 98 years old. He was still treating patients at the time of his death. One day Grandpa said he was tired, and he wanted to rest. He lay down on the bed and because I was visiting him at the time, he asked me to massage him. Grandpa told me, "Remember to put your head into your education and be the best at you can. Whatever you do make sure you are the top in your position. Be the best of the best at whatever you do. All of your aunts and uncles, they do not care for you like I do, so you need to stand on your own feet." Grandpa then called for my aunt and told her that he thought he did not have much time left. He told my aunt to call a family meeting. The whole family arrived as soon as possible, and they gathered around Grandpa. He told us all, "I am very tired, it's time to go." He told my aunt to take care of me, that I was honest and good, and to be fair to me because he would not be here anymore. Grandpa then took his last breath.

Grandpa left a generous will. He owned a lot of land and houses. He left me a rare gold watch, which he purchased when he was in Paris in 1910, as well as his medical school class ring. My favorite aunt wanted the gold watch, but Grandpa had wanted me to have it. Grandpa was a big influence on me when he was alive and unbeknownst to me at the time, would play a big part in my future.

After four years of law school, at age 20, I took the bar exam. I passed the exam, and then went straight to Ginaymo Military Base for a selective military training program. Since I wanted to be an attorney for military personnel, I was simultaneously training to be a soldier and training to be a lawyer. The two-year program was like what West Point cadets go through. A typical day began at 5 a.m. with jogging. We then did military training for three hours. This included shooting guns, how to use radio communication, and how to drive tanks. I happened to be a very good sharpshooter and I enjoyed this part of my training. It probably had something to do with the aim I developed when I was taught by Sergeant Thommasane to throw knives at a target and to shoot a gun. The most difficult thing we had to do during training was to crawl under barbed wire while being shot at with real bullets. We could not raise our heads up during this exercise or we would risk being shot. There was also parachute training. While I did not mind this exercise, my friend, Bounchanh Nakanthi, did not enjoy it at all. I knew Bounchanh from high school back in Vientiane. We had first met while we were both playing on our school soccer teams. I was #7 and Bounchanh was #9. When I played soccer, I tended to be all over the place on the field, and Bounchanh used to think I was the better player because of that habit. Bounchanh was in a different training class out of Sayabury, a province in Laos, but he had training at the same time as me. Bounchanh was very slight in build. When his parachute opened and he landed, now it was him who was all over the place; because of his slight build, he was dragged across several rice fields.

The political and military landscape in Laos during my military training was getting more dangerous by the day. The NVA tried to infiltrate Longchang, Auttapeu and Pakchong, parts of Laos that were located close to North Vietnam. There was an instance where a communist spy tried to get into the military school. My friend Bounchanh and I were working as guards on the military base one night to keep an eye out for this spy, and we stopped him. We had learned about the spy because we would send out two or three of our soldiers to ask the villagers about suspicious civilians near the base. We would earn the villagers trust by supplying them with things when we visited, like rice, vegetables, and medicine. The villagers helped us identify the spy because they alerted us that some men came into the village and asked for donations of supplies. This was a clear giveaway that these people wanted to get food to supply the NVA.

After five hours of military training, from 10 a.m. to 5 p.m., I would train to be a military attorney and would learn how to try cases. In 1967, I graduated third in a class of 21 with a rank of second lieutenant. After graduation, I took, and passed, another exam to become a member of the military bar.

Not only did my father have a front row view of how the NVA fought, but he also saw firsthand how the CIA operated. During my military school training, my father mentioned to me for the first time that he and his younger brother were working with the CIA. According to my father, the CIA was helping Laos fight against the communists. The spy agency was supplying Laos with money, ammunition, weapons, food, clothing, uniforms and medical supplies. My father and uncle made sure all of the incoming supplies were accounted for. My father also retrieved money from the CIA, which was stuffed into anywhere from five to nine duffle bags, and delivered it to the soldiers on the frontlines every month. The process was very straightforward. An American airplane dropped the money off at the military base which was located at the Wattay International Airport in Vientiane. A man named "Officer James" delivered the U.S. dollars to the Bank of Vientiane. My father's sister was the owner of the bank, and she oversaw the conversion of the money to kip, the local currency. Officer James and other military personnel brought the converted currency back to the base where my father signed for it. My father then transferred the money to a helicopter, and it was flown and dispersed to the soldiers on the front lines. Officer James and his colleague "Officer David" clearly were important people. My father also once met with Henry Kissinger at the base. It was a very secure operation on the base. My father had 10 to 15 armed soldiers with him to handle the money. There were never any attempts to steal money by the communists or criminals. Once the money left the base, however, security became an issue. There were times during disbursement of money to soldiers that the NVA attacked and then money had to be taken back to Vientiane. When soldiers were killed in battle before they could be paid, my father was responsible for bringing the money to the soldiers' survivors. During this time, my father had complete confidence and trust in the CIA and the U.S. military during the war.

No sooner than I finished military school, it was time to test my confidence and trust in what I was trained to do. In early 1968, I was ordered to report the city of Laognam, south of Laos, in the province of Auttapeu. My father had previously fought against the NVA in the same area. Heavy fighting was taking place near a tall mountain called Phoulouang, which also served as a satellite center for the Lao government for communication. Before I reported for duty, my mother was very nervous for me. Even though she was the wife of a soldier, she did not want her oldest son to go to the battle. My mother went so far as to ask my father, "Because of your position in the military you could influence where he goes or does not go. Please send him someplace else that is not as dangerous." My father was unmoved and said, "If he is afraid, he should not be a soldier. He committed himself to be a soldier, and vowed to protect the King and our country, so he should not be afraid." My father turned to me and gave me some simple advice: "If it is not your time to die, you won't." For some reason, I was not afraid. I expected I would see fighting, bombs, gunshots, and death. I was prepared for battle.

I was a second lieutenant with 200 men under my command. Several helicopters took us to the top of

Phoulouang mountain. Each helicopter could carry 25 men. The air transport from Vientiane airport to Phoulouang mountain took about one hour. These transports took place during the day time because we knew that the NVA slept during the day, attacked at sundown and kept attacking through the night. We arrived at Phoulouang at about 4 or 5 in the afternoon. I met with Captain Sert who informed me that he had started out with 100 men on the mountain, but he had lost a lot of them already. Knowing this was my first tour of duty, and probably worried that I was scared, Captain Sert explained to me that it was normal to be nervous before my first battle experience. He advised me to do my best to be calm, to take a deep breath and not panic. He said, "We are the leaders. We have to be strong and tough. When the sun sets, the attacking will begin. Make sure all of your men are alert."

As Captain Sert promised, at around 6 or 7 p.m. when it started getting dark, the NVA attacked. It was an eruption of big guns shooting and big bombs exploding. It all sounded like popcorn popping and thunderous earthquakes going off at the same time. I tried to calm myself down even though there were bombs and gunfire all around me. Then when the fight came to us, everything happened fast... faster than I ever imagined. There was no time to be nervous or to think of anything other than: if I don't kill the enemy, they will kill me. I was shooting my weapon, and it seemed like I was killing many NVA soldiers all at once. When I ran out of bullets, which also happened very fast, I killed NVA soldiers with the bayonet at the end of my gun. I could not believe that the only wound I suffered during the first battle was a scratch on my arm.

Many of us took positions in curved trenches which were dug around the mountain. A bomb dropped into the trench near where I was. Six or seven of my men were killed in the blast. The power of blast blew me and a few others right out of the hole and into the air. Unlike the parachute jumps I did during my military training, there was not going to be a soft landing. When I hit the ground, it felt like my chest compressed and the wind was knocked out of me. I had only been on the battlefield for a short while but it felt much longer.

During my first battle, I also served as a medic for the wounded soldiers. I ran from trench to trench, checking on my men. I carried soldiers to a safe spot before tending to their wounds. I gave wounded soldiers shots to numb the pain or before I removed bullets. My uniform was soaked with blood from doing this work. Many of my fellow soldiers got blown up by bombs. It was one of my jobs to put them, or what was left of them, in body bags.

Actual battle was harder to take than I had ever imagined. I had to forget about myself and focus on being a leader and taking care of my fellow soldiers. I was also angry at the enemy for killing and wounding my men. They outnumbered us and seemed to be all around us like a never-ending trail of ants. In all the noise and confusion, I had to focus my troops on shooting at as many of the enemy soldiers as they could. Our goal was to save the territory and whatever fear I had before the battle had been wiped away. Our mentality always had to be: it's either them or me.

We always had to be on high alert for the many dangers of war. For example, there were many booby traps that the NVA laid for us. They would dig a hole and place sharp bamboo sticks on the bottom of the hole. They would cover the hole with leaves and twigs. When soldiers walked over it, they would fall into the hole and get impaled by bamboo sticks. My squad had specialists who had experience spotting these traps. Not only would we have to pay attention to the dangers on the ground, but we had to be on the lookout for the dangers in the trees. The NVA would sleep on top of the trees during the day in hammocks. We would assign soldiers the task of looking up when they walked. If they spotted NVA up in the trees, they would shoot them. We would sneak in our sleep during the day like the NVA did, and we had soldiers assigned to guard those who slept.

Unlike the military men in Laos, American troops fighting in Vietnam were not well trained about this sleeping habit of the NVA. Also, American troops were unfamiliar with the jungle terrain and, more importantly, the mindset of the NVA. Our mutual enemy was cold and deadly. They had absolutely no fear of death in the name of their cause. If one NVA soldier died, another would step over their body and continue the fight. They even used dead bodies of their fellow soldiers to shield them or to use the dead as ladders to climb over any obstacles. While American soldiers could try to beat the NVA physically, it was a more difficult fight to beat them mentally because the enemy did not care if they died. As far as we Laotians were concerned, we knew the communists wanted to take over our country, the country we all loved. We would lose our freedom if the communists won. As a result of this reality, we were willing to die to protect our country.

The battle at Phoulouang was heavy and long. The weather during the battle was always the same: foggy and cold in the morning, with a little rain. Our standard rations supplied by the American military were hot dogs and rice in bags that had to be warmed up. We were also given energy bars for when we were walking for long periods of time. We certainly needed all the energy we could get. For the next two weeks, nighttime was filled with nonstop shooting and explosions. Daytime was relatively quiet, and we could get a little sleep here and there. What kept us from sleeping, however, was that we were so heavily outnumbered by our enemy. During one battle, 3,000 to 4,000 enemy soldiers raced up from both sides of the mountain and trapped us. There was absolutely no escape. On one side of us was a rocky cliff and the other side of us was a hillside with trees as big as the ones in Yosemite. The enemy kept swarming up from both sides. My soldiers and I kept shooting our weapons until they turned red from heat and could not shoot any more. Then we had to grab another gun and keep shooting until that one became too hot to handle. We had to resort to using all of our grenades to keep the enemy at bay. The NVA were close to getting to the top of the mountain, to kill us all and to raise their flag. Captain Sert was riddled with many bullets from an AK-47. He knew he was going to die. I kneeled by him and he said to me, "I know I'm not going to make it but don't be afraid. You need to do your best, do not let them take over this mountain. You will need to fight and lead your men until your last breath." Captain Sert took his last breath soon after that.

During a break in the attack, I could not think of rest or sleep. I was worried about my men and was afraid they would get slaughtered. But my men were battle tested before I took command. I had to let them know I was going to keep leading them and to keep fighting. I ran from trench to trench to make sure they were awake and had food. Like Captain Sert insisted, I had to make sure they all were on high alert. We hardly slept during these battles for the next week. I only had 33 men alive in my unit, and there were only 40 men left from Captain Sert's unit. Against all odds, my troops put up a relentless fight. We were aided by air support and strikes from U.S. forces who were based in Thailand. Between our will to win on the ground, and the precision strikes from F-15 and F-16 fighter jets that destroyed the big trees providing cover for the NVA, we won the battle. Now, even though the war in Laos was called a "Secret War," it was no secret that we were supported by U.S. forces. While U.S. forces could not set foot in our country, they could support our forces by air and with supplies.

I knew for certain we had won the battle at Phoulouang because when the fighting stopped there were no NVA soldiers to be found in the vicinity. I checked myself to see if I had been injured. All I had suffered was a scratch and many slashes that just cut my uniform. Even though I could not recall how many men I had killed, I could not stop thinking about how many men had been killed on both sides. My team checked the dead bodies, looking for any NVA survivors. There were none. What we discovered, however, was that the reason we were outnumbered and overwhelmed by the enemy was that Chinese communist soldiers were supporting the NVA. We noticed some dead communist soldiers wore the Chinese military uniforms made of thin cotton. We also saw the dog tags and photos of their families in their pockets were Chinese. While looking at the photos of the families the dead NVA and Chinese soldiers reminded me of the fragility of life in war, I had to remind myself again that it was either them or me.

CHAPTER FIVE

Following the battle of Phoulouang, I was promoted from Second Lieutenant to Captain. At that time, my father was on the front lines at Xiangkhouang, fighting another battle. When I came home, I called the military base in Vientiane. Personnel connected me by radio to my father on the battlefield so I could let him know I was OK. I then began a 10-day break from combat.

At the beginning of my break, I went with a group of 11 friends to a Buddhist temple called Wat Thamhao in Vientiane. Like sixty to seventy percent of the Laotian people, my family was Buddhist. I became more religious once I joined the military. When men went to battle, they needed something to believe in, something to make them feel "protected" from getting killed. After all, the survival rate in war was 50%. When my friends mentioned they knew about a great Buddha Master, I agreed to go with them because I wanted whatever extra protection I could have.

The Buddha monk we went to see was named Master Boundam Sacksith. Master Sacksith was in his 60's, and he was known for his special power to help people who believed in him. He only selected followers who were able to strictly follow the Five Precepts of Buddhism. To be a monk, one had to live by 220 rules so I naively figured how tough could it be to only live by five! The five precepts I had to swear to abide by were the following:

1. "I undertake the training-precept to abstain from onslaught on breathing beings."

2. "I undertake the training-precept to abstain from taking what is not given."

3. "I undertake the training-precept to abstain from misconduct concerning sense-pleasures."

4. "I undertake the training-precept to abstain from false speech."

5. "I undertake the training-precept to abstain from alcoholic drink or drugs that are an opportunity for heedlessness."

The rules translated to mean that I could not kill any living thing, I could not steal, I could not commit adultery, I could not lie or gossip (unless it was needed to survive), and I could not partake in intoxication through alcohol, drugs or other means. I did think it odd that while a Buddhist monk was prohibited from killing anybody, I was allowed to do so as a solider fighting for my country.

After Master explained the rules, he asked my friends and I, "Who is able to accept all the rules? Be warned that if you accept and cannot do it, it will cost you your life in the war zone." My friends admitted they could not strictly follow the rules, even though they seriously considered doing so. I was the only one who promised that I could live by the rules. I wanted to make the commitment to have whatever protection I could have while I was on the battlefield.

Master then invited me to stay in the temple for the nine-day ritual. I had to ask my father and the military for permission to go through with the ritual. Buddhist tradition holds that before a Buddhist man turns 25 years old, he must serve under a Buddhist monk to pay back his ancestors and parents. This ritual allows the man's parents to go to Heaven. The Lao military usually gave permission for men to go become a Buddhist monk. My father went through a similar ritual with a different Master, so he gave his permission for me to do the ritual.

My family observed Buddhism, but we were not strict. My Grandpa had a Buddhist altar in his house. On the altar was a photo of his parents' picture on it. On a special day, Grandpa would pay respect to his parents. He would stand, put his fists together and bowed three times to the photo. As an adult, my father practiced Buddhism when he could; he meditated and said prayers to the Buddha. When I was a boy, I had attended temple which was near our house in Luang Prabang. My mother prepared offerings and food for the local Buddha monk at the temple.

On the first day of the ritual, Master shaved my head, gave me a white outfit to wear, then he started to pray and chant in Sri Lanka/Sanskirt language. Using a small sharp knife and sesame seed oil, Master wrote on my body, like he was etching tattoos on me from head to toe. What Master tattooed on my body were rules to protect me. The rules were written in the Bali Sanskirt language (the original Indian language), and nobody could read the words except Master himself. Every five to 10 minutes, Master would pour warm water on my body to wash away all the blood... but it did not wash away the pain!

Master and I would then chant for six hours a day, only breaking to eat and drink. I was allowed to sleep at night but I was in too much pain from all of the knife cuts on my body. I developed an intense fever for six days, probably because of those opens wounds. Master brewed a medicinal tea in a coconut shell and fed it to me. After six days, the pain and fever went away due to the mysterious medicine in the coconut shell.

On the ninth day of the ritual, Master pulled out another sharp knife, which was 12 inches long and looked like a butcher knife. Master said he was going to test me. It took all of my focus to prepare for the pain. Master chopped at my back a couple of times. I heard the knife whip past my back, but the blade did not seem to touch my skin. Master said the test was over. He told me that whenever I was about to go into battle during the war, I needed to pray and think of Master, pick up dirt from the Mother of Earth, put a pinch on my head and pray, "Mother of Earth please protect me." This would make sure that Master would protect me from any weapon touching my skin. It was a superstition that many soldiers who were Buddhists believed in. I certainly had no doubt about what my Master told me.

After the ritual with my Buddha Master, I came home to Vientiane and I received new orders: I was going off to fight in Khe Sanh. When I got the order to go to Khe Sanh, I called my father again and told him the news. My father said Khe Sanh was going to be worse than the first battle I had just fought in. My father had gotten the word from his military people that the NVA and Chinese communists had swept into Khe Sanh like a big wave and were already on the ground. My father also mentioned the CIA to me. He said the CIA needed military men from Laos to assist them in fighting the communists. He also said, "If they need help it would be good for you and our country for you to help them when the time comes."

Khe Sanh was strategically a very important area. Not only was it only seven miles from Laos, but it was part of the Ho Chi Minh Trail, which the NVA used to transport weapons, troops and supplies into South Vietnam. The strategy, then, was for us to fly over Khe Sanh in a C130 plane and then parachute in because NVA and Chinese communists were already on the ground. Once on the ground, danger would be around every corner. The terrain was a valley with big mountains and many large trees. Our enemy would have plenty of cover. We were bluntly advised to prepare for the worst.

In the winter of 1968, I boarded the C130 plane. As one of five captains leading 500 men, I kept all fear and concerns to myself, and put on a brave face. Each C130 plane carried 50 men to our destination. During the hour and a half flight from Vientiane to Khe Sanh, there was minimal talk among the men. Some sat with their heads bowed and prayed silently. I prayed, too. I thought about my Buddha Master and asked him to protect me. Most of us touched the Buddhas that we wore on gold chains around our necks. I wore nine of them; one was given to me by my Master, two more given to me by Sergeant Thommasane and the rest were given to me by my father. The significance of wearing the Buddhas was that they would help protect me when I was in the danger zone. There were other soldiers who merely looked at photos of their families that they kept in their uniforms. I also carried a photo of my parents in addition to my Buddhas. What went unsaid was that we were all prepared to die for our country. This could be the last day of our lives but if it was in the name of defeating communism, then so be it.

Our C130 reached the drop zone at around 12:00 p.m. In broad daylight, we jumped out of the plane at 3,000 feet. As the troop leader, I jumped out first. My men followed one by one. The next thing I knew, I saw men next to me getting shot in mid-air. The NVA started their offensive as soon as they saw us parachuting down. I heard bullets from anti-aircraft guns zipping through the air and hitting everyone around me. Fine red mist sprayed out around me like fireworks as each man got riddled with bullets. While the sight was horrifying and my body trembled, I had the strange feeling I was being protected. As soon as I landed on the ground, I picked up the dirt and put it on my head before I started to fight, just like my Buddha Master had instructed me.

So began one of the longest and bloodiest battles in the war. From the moment I dropped down to the ground, I fought until late into the night. Combat with the enemy was hand to hand much of the time, but with knife and bayonet I killed my enemy before they could kill me. My training was keeping me alive so far. When darkness fell, the danger escalated. We had to crawl on the ground to make as little noise as possible. When we attacked or were attacked, the only way to differentiate one side from another in close combat was from the feel of the uniforms we grappled with. Our uniforms were made of material like Americans uniforms; they were 100% cotton but of a higher and sturdier quality. The NVA and Chinese communist uniforms, on the other hand, were flimsier and more slippery. Even though the enemy's uniforms were inferior, there were more of their uniformed soldiers to deal with on the battlefield because they outnumbered us many times over... and they were beating us badly.

All of us who served in the Royal Lao Army military had to learn basic field medic procedures. However, I was chosen to learn more advanced procedures because of my medical background from helping Grandpa when I was a boy. I was able to administering IV's and perform basic surgery to remove bullets and shrapnel. These extra skills were something I was competent at and not all captains could perform them. My main goal was to stop the bleeding as soon as possible then get the injured soldier to a safe hiding place There was usually not much time to help because I also had to protect myself.

Sometimes all the skills and time in the world could not save lives. There was a time during the battle that we were getting slaughtered by the enemy. We were literally running out of men to keep fighting. One of the soldiers that served with me was named Khampheng. He was originally from Savannakhet City. During a battle, Khampheng was shot, and the injury sent him stumbling onto a land mine. The explosion blew his leg clean off below the knee. The rest of his body was pierced with shrapnel. I rushed over to help him however I could. As he lay there on the ground, bloodied and in agonizing pain, he mustered the strength to tell me, "Captain, do not give up. Keep fighting for us. You need to fight to chase them out of our country. If we do not have enough men, then go back and get more. We need to get rid of the communists." Khampheng knew he was dying. He said if he was reincarnated, he wanted to be a soldier again. I told him I wanted him to go to Heaven and be in peace. I promised him that if I survived, I would go back and bring more men. I also promised to fight til the last man. In a few minutes, Khampheng nodded, became quiet and minutes later, he died.

The fighting at Khe Sanh continued and only became more intense. We were sleep deprived but there was no time to feel tired. During the battle on that second day, not only was I left with 71 men to fight thousands of Chinese communists, but I also got shot. Bullets hit me below the calf on my left leg and behind the inside of my right thigh. In the heat of battle, I did not realize I had been shot at first. I kept shooting my weapon. I then felt like there was cold water running down my leg. I looked and saw the blood soaking my pant leg. I dragged myself to a big tree nearby for cover. I tried to treat my own wounds, but I was losing blood very quickly. I thought I would not survive because my wounds prevented me from moving quickly. Also, I knew that the enemy bullets were laced with a toxic material. If my wounds were not treated quickly, I would be poisoned. Some of my men who saw me get shot ran over and guarded me as I treated my wounds. I sat up against the tree, shot myself up with a syringe filled with morphine to numb my wounds then wrapped the wound with a bandage. One of my radio men called the helicopter to come in and pick up me along with 4 or 5 other men who were also injured. It took about 45 minutes for the helicopter to arrive. The small amount of morphine I injected myself with started to wear off. The pain overwhelmed me so much that I was not sure if I was going to make it out alive. I thought, however, if I died, I would at least die with pride. During the helicopter ride out of the battle zone, even though other men were all severely injured, they spoke of wanting to go back and fight the communists again after being healed. I had the same goal.

I was admitted to a hospital in Thailand in the city of Udon. My wounds were so serious that I was hospitalized for two months. Military personnel at the hospital contacted my father to let him know I was injured but that I would recover. During May of 1968, I was still in the hospital and had almost recuperated from my injuries. A commander came to the hospital and asked us who wanted to go back to Khe Sanh for another tour of duty. Everyone who was in the hospital who had been wounded during the first battle of Khe Sanh wanted to go back and fight. We all wanted to honor the memory of our fellow soldiers who sacrificed their lives and we wanted to fight to keep our country out of the hands of the communists.

Before we left for our second tour of duty in Khe Sanh, we got our supplies from the U.S. military. The supplies were delivered to us from the U.S. bases in Thailand. Instead of being flown in by plane, a few hundred of us piled into helicopters to make the journey back to Khe Sanh. There were, on average, 12 men per helicopter. We were dropped off at a low level. Khe Sanh mountain used to be green but after all the months of fighting, the trees were now all burned down and it looked like a "bald" mountain. There was another tall mountain a good distance away which American troops used for a communication post. The NVA wanted to conquer this area for strategic reasons so there were many fights to win this territory. Just like my first drop at Khe Sanh, the area was heavily surrounded by NVA. Like before, the fighting began immediately.

We fought for two days straight on our way to protect the American communication base. Some battles were better for us than others. Once again, I watched our troops get mowed down in battles where we were badly outnumbered. Many of my men were gravely wounded but often we could not call in medical helicopters or treat the men's injuries because of the fierce and constant fighting. We needed help and we needed it fast.

I called the Udon base from a special line for our soldiers and asked for aerial support. Using a map I always carried with me, I was able to communicate to the base where the bombing area was located. I then relayed information to all surrounding units to clear the area before the bombings began. Sometimes we would also fire off warning shots to alert our men that aerial bombings were on the way. Usually, the bombings would take place 30 minutes after I placed the order. Unless there was bad weather, the bombings would always be carried out. While the Soviet Union and the Chinese supplied small plane cover for the NVA, we had air support from American B52 bombers as well as F15 and F16 fighter jets. By this time, I was down to my last 44 men. Fortunately, the constant and precise bombing by American planes evened out the battlefield. Thousands of NVA were killed from the bombings. We soon returned to the offensive on the ground, prevented the NVA from taking the base and chased the enemy survivors away. After 10 days of fighting, we were finally victorious.

Despite our victory, there was still much to be unhappy about. The Royal Lao Army lost between 5,000 and 6,000 soldiers. 71 men who I had fought with during the first battle at Khe Sanh, with whom I returned to fight again with, had all been killed. Those of us who survived had to patrol the Khe Sanh base, count the number of dead NVA, and then dig holes to bury the bodies. It was during this unpleasant task that I discovered dead NVA soldiers who were chained up to big anti-aircraft guns. This was how these soldiers were treated by their communist leaders. We did find some surviving NVA soldiers. These survivors were sent to jail in Vientiane with the purpose to later trade them for Laotian prisoners. These negotiations were carried out by our Prime Minister.

There were some instances of spying, where NVA soldiers pretended to be Laotian. They dressed in on our style of clothes and tried to pass themselves off as one of us. These men were carefully questioned: who are you, what is your military ID number, what is your code number? If that person could not answer quickly and correctly, we would know for sure they were NVA and they would be shot. Also, NVA and Chinese communists had different accents than us so their voices would usually give them away. Most of the time, however, the enemy prisoners were killed especially when it was discovered that NVA prisoners who were traded for Lao prisoners came back to the battlefield.

When I returned home, I was awarded a medal from the Royal Family. It was a gold medal of honor of a three headed elephant called "Banjamaphon" which means "Order of the Million Elephants and the White Parasol." The 44 men who served under me, and had also survived the two battles of Khe Sanh, also received medals. It was a big ceremony in Vientiane; my entire family was in attendance, as well as several generals who served alongside my father. Other soldiers received well-earned medal that day in recognition of their service in other battles. I still have my medal to this day. But that day's ceremony was not the end of my military career. Far from it.

CHAPTER SIX

After the battle at Khe Sanh, I stayed in Vientiane about two weeks. I then received orders to report to fight another battle in the Southern province of Auttapeu. That part of Laos was very mountainous. The airplanes and helicopters could not transport soldiers and supplies in the direct area, so they had to be dropped off in the lowlands near the villages. It was a two day walk to get to the fighting area because of the terrain and elevation. We also had to stay off the roads and stick to traveling through the jungles.

Auttapeu was populated with tribal people who were called Akha. My troops and I marched along, patrolling the route to the village. There were 7 or 8 villages in the area, and each one was about 25 to 30 minutes apart. The smaller villages had 30 huts and the bigger villages had over 100 huts. When we approached a village, there was usually a fence around it to protect the villagers from dangerous animals. The main entrance was identified by an arch, with five steps up and five steps down leading into the center of the village. Visitors were greeted by a pile of dirt that was about two feet high. Near the pile of dirt was a sign written in Laotian. The message was that anyone wanting to enter the village had to ask for permission from the village's protector spirit before one could enter. The request had to be loud enough for someone in the village to hear it. There was a big hut in the center of village, which served as a meeting area for village meetings. When villagers saw people from the outside, the leader of the village would ask them if they asked permission to enter. If one did not ask permission, that person had to sacrifice something, like an animal, to the protector spirit. Otherwise, the belief was that an offending person would bring sickness or death to the village. I had to follow this ritual in every village I came to. When I arrived with my troops, I routinely announced that I was Captain Ratanakone, that we were the royal military men and we asked permission to enter your village. Once we were allowed into the village, I would ask the villagers if the NVA had come by asking for food. The way the NVA worked was very harsh. If they got what they asked for, they would leave the village alone. If the village did not give the NVA what they asked for, they would burn the village down.

Besides noticing where villages were obviously burned down, there was another way for me to keep track of where the enemy had been. One benefit of

Auttapeu's mountainous area was that the land had rich farming soil. The NVA planted cassava plant, which is a root like a potato or a yam. The enemy would plant cassava in the farm areas of the villages. The trick was to tell if a local villager planted the cassava or if the NVA planted it. The way to tell the difference was that if villagers planted it, they would pull the weeds and keep the plant clean. However, if the NVA planted it, there would be weeds showing. If we came across cassava plants with weeds, we would destroy it and deprive our enemy of their food source.

The NVA made sure to do whatever they could to hurt us as we traveled through the jungle. While we were trained about what types of traps to look out for, it was always challenging to spot them. We had to walk very carefully, and it slowed our travel time significantly. The NVA were generally not very big people. They would bury a hole, lie down in it, cover themselves up with leaves and bamboo sticks and wait to ambush us. They would also place sharp bamboo sticks at the bottom of a hole so if someone fell into the hole they would be impaled. I had the misfortune of falling into one of these holes once but just missed being hurt by the bamboo spears. One time, when we passed through a village called Phapeung, we had two or three scouts who made sure it was safe for the rest of the team to enter. One of the scouts stepped on a landmine. Half of his lower right leg was blown clear off below the knee. A communication man radioed me to report the attack. I gave the order to give the injured soldier a morphine shot to help his pain and then called the base to transport the injured scout out of there.

While passing through another village, one of my men named Khamy was on his first patrol. Khamy had just graduated from his military training class. He knew that he always had to watch the person walking in front of him and try to step in the exact spot they stepped in to avoid stepping on a landmine. Careful as he was, Khamy took a step with his left leg, heard the unmistakable click, froze and yelled, "I stepped on a bomb!" Now every one of us froze. It was as if we all had one foot on the bomb as well. I ordered Khamy not lift up his left leg. If he lifted that leg the bomb would explode. Khamy was very nervous and shaky, so I ordered another solider had to keep pressure on Khamy's leg so he would not lift it. Meanwhile, I dropped to my knees and started digging away the leaves and the dirt. At first, everyone must have thought I was digging our collective grave. But I knew how to dismantle the bomb. From my military training, I knew it was a

Chinese-made bomb. Once I exposed the bomb that the NVA had camouflaged with leaves and dirt, I used a little knife, turned the cap of the bomb and used the knife to lock the device so it could not click. I then dismantled the parts and destroyed it. We all breathed a sigh of relief, especially Khamy. He could not thank me enough. I was reminded, as I had to remind all of my men, that every step in war is a matter of life or death.

Another time at Auttapeu, we were marching down a path between two mountains during a patrol mission near a river. One of my best friends told me that he was hungry. We had been fighting for two or three days straight, and all we had to eat were energy bars. I was concerned that the NVA were positioned on top of the mountain so they could see us coming through. I was worried that if they were waiting for us, we should not put anything in our mouth. I believed that if one of us opened our mouth to eat something, we would be vulnerable to being shot. I told my friend, "Wait. Don't eat, don't eat. We are not in the safe zone yet." My friend's hunger was too great, and he could not wait any longer. He ran towards a big tree for cover, and unwrapped an energy bar. As he was about to put it in his mouth, a shot rang out from where the NVA were positioned. A bullet hit him in the right side of the chest. He called for me, I ran over to him and saw right away that his wound was fatal. My friend said that he knew he was dying. He cried and screamed that he missed home, and he wanted to see his mother and father. He kept talking about his home and family until he died. To get away from the ambush, my men and I had to jump in the water and let the river carry us downstream to momentary safety. Sadly, because of our retreat, we were unable to get my dead friend's remains home for a proper funeral.

The area in and around Phouloung mountain is where many of the Auttapeu battles took place. Based on our previous setbacks, I changed tactics and tried to determine where the enemy were sleeping in the daytime. I communicated with my men on the mountain and was informed that the NVA slept in large groups in the same area. I ordered my men up on the mountain to shoot down smoke bombs 50 feet to the right or 100 feet to the left until they hit the right target. When the smoke bombs hit the mark, the NVA scattered from the smoke bombs and then our men would shoot them. We would wait for the NVA to run out of bullets as they shot into the smoky distance and then we would attack them. The NVA would sometimes blow a whistle to get their troops to prepare to attack. There would then be an attacking rallying cry of, "Arizo arizo!" These sounds would alert us as to where the NVA were positioned. In other cases, when the NVA knocked a stick to knock against bamboo, that was a signal for them to retreat. They would also sometimes make a bird-call type sound to signal a withdrawal. If I heard any of these kinds of sounds, I would order my men to keep shooting at the NVA because I knew we had them on the run. I discovered later that the U.S. military were not aware of these NVA signals. Had they been, they would have had more success attacking the NVA. As for us, whenever we knew that the NVA pulled back, our troops would shoot them and chase them until they were dead or stopped fighting.

Even though my 535 troops were outnumbered by the 2000 NVA troops, after 10 days of battle, we were able to force the NVA out of Auttapeu. I was very battle-tested by now, but I realized that we were outmanned by our enemy and that was not going to change any time soon. As I walked through the area after the battle, I saw and smelled death with every step. I felt an even greater responsibility to do my best to keep my men alive. I also had to remind myself to be even more calm, cautious and tougher in order to continue to lead my men and country to victory.

CHAPTER SEVEN

After the victory in Auttapeu, I returned to
Vientiane for about three weeks. However, there was
little time for a relaxing break. I trained our current
personnel about what I had learned on the battlefield and
provided intelligence about our enemy to new troops that
were about to be sent into battle. I taught these new
soldiers what the daily life of the NVA was like, especially
the activities of the NVA in the villages. I taught them to
respect the villagers' beliefs and customs so they could
earn their respect and trust and win their hearts. The
communists would always lie to the villagers by telling
them, "If you all become communists, everyone will be
rich, and you will have everything you want." However, if
the villagers did not do what the NVA wanted or if they
lied to the NVA, their village would be destroyed. I taught
the new soldiers the differences between the crops
planted by the villagers and the crops planted by the NVA.
I taught them to pay attention to every detail so that they
could identify when something was abnormal. While I was
teaching new soldiers, I also attended some classes and
training for myself. At the end of these three weeks in
1968, I received new orders to report to fight in Sepon.

Sepon was located near the Ho Chi Minh Trail. Lowland Lao villagers lived in this area in villages that had between 100 and 200 huts. I marched my troops on patrol through the area, always trying to gather intelligence to find out when the NVA came around to collect food, what they said, and what they did. As was always the case, the NVA would burn a village to the ground if they did not get food, supplies and cooperation. I made sure to let the villagers know that, unlike the communists, they did not need to be afraid of us. We were on their side, and that we were there to help if any suspicious activities occurred.

We were frequently attacked by the NVA during our patrols. Sepon was considered a "failed zone" for the United States. They could not provide their usual air strike support to help us there because NVA soldiers were concentrated all over the two large mountains, armed with plenty of anti-aircraft machine guns. The best I could do was use my binoculars to report back to base how far apart the anti-aircraft machine guns were positioned. We were then able to send men in to attack the enemy position. Once again, we discovered that the soldiers we killed were chained to the anti-aircraft machine guns. That was simply the philosophy of the communists; their guns were more important than their people.

The NVA had a clear manpower advantage, and they used those soldiers to burn down many villages. We launched an attack on the NVA after they burned down a village. We needed to call the base to get more support on the ground. Even though 12 of my men were injured, no one died. Meanwhile, we killed 30 NVA soldiers. A few years later in 1971, there was a bigger battle in Sepon called Operation Lantern 719 which involved American and South Vietnamese soldiers, but I did not fight in that battle.

The next battle I was involved in was at a mountain called Phou Lek. "Phou Lek" meant "iron mountain." With 289 soldiers under my command, we fought the NVA for the next 26 days. As usual, we were badly outnumbered, and were up against around 3,000 to 4,000 NVA troops. By the end of the battle, the dead were scattered all over the mountainous terrain. Once again, we had succeeded in chasing the NVA out of the area. I returned home to Vientiane with 122 surviving members of my unit.

I was not in Vientiane for long when I returned to do battle in the old capital city of Luang Prabang. The inhabitants had all moved out. We moved in and waited for the NVA to arrive. As soon we saw them, we attacked. It was non-stop mayhem and gunfire. There was a time during the battle that we were shooting at each other while taking cover under a house. But that melee did not last long because the NVA burned the house down. Even though we had killed a few hundred NVA, casualties on our side were racking up; 40 of our men were killed, and 23 were injured. In the middle of the battle, I had to treat my men's wounds and pull out the dead men. To make matters worse, I received word from our spies that NVA reinforcement troops were on the way, so we had better pull back and retreat. I only had 255 men left. Instead of evacuating, I called for backup. An old friend of mine came in to help save the day.

Bounchanh Nakanthi, my friend from high school and officer's training school, was serving honorably in the war as a captain. Bounchanh came in to support my troops and together we chased the NVA out of Luang Prabang and captured 29 enemy soldiers. I interrogated 13 of the prisoners. These prisoners were uncooperative so, as I had been trained to do, I resorted to force. I hit the NVA with a gun and demanded, "If you do not answer us and tell us the truth, we will kill you." Finally, they spoke, and they all generally answered the same way.

They said they had to come to fight in Laos to help their country. They said that they had always been told that because Americans helped Laos, then they also had to fight against Laos because America was the enemy. They said they were forced to be soldiers, and that they had to fight because Americans killed their parents. They admitted that communists would hold a soldiers' family hostage to force the men to fight and force the women to transport food and supplies. The captured soldiers also admitted that the communists wanted to take over Laos, and they were ordered to win this battle at all costs. After the interrogations, the NVA soldiers were imprisoned in Vientiane.

I moved on with 465 soldiers in a unit known as the 333rd to fight the next battle in Nambark, which was located in northern Laos. There was no direct road to travel from Luang Prabang to Nambark so we traveled 18 hours by boat along the Namou River. Once we arrived in Nambark, we set out to patrol the 30 to 40 villages in and around the area. When the NVA had previously invaded Nambark, the villagers became refugees, therefore, most of the villages were empty. The NVA moved into the villages with about 20,000 to 30,000 troops. There was only one way in and out of the village and the NVA would usually arrive during the daytime. We surrounded the area in such a way that the NVA would not know we were there. When we knew for sure that the NVA were situated inside the village, with their guard down a bit, we attacked them and burned down the village. The villages were made up of huts, so they were easy to burn down. We were giving them a taste of their own medicine now by burning down the village with them in it.

Soon after our latest victory, during the summer of 1968, I moved south to fight the NVA in the city district of Khammouan. Khammouan was an even more dangerous area because it was located close to North Vietnam. The battle took place near an area with many tall mountains called Pha Home, also known as Phou Soung. I received an intelligence report from General Sulith Pakvee and General Chao Sayavong Savang in Luang Prabang that spies from our side had blended in with the local villagers. These spies learned that the NVA would pass through the village and then go to a cave. This cave was in the mountain region in the Meuangmahaxay District. This cave looked more like an old volcano with a big hole on top, and the bottom was an even bigger area that resembled a cave. The area was large enough to house 3,000 to 4,000 NVA soldiers. Strategically, there was only one way for the enemy to enter and leave this area. As was their preferred habit, the NVA move at night and sleep there during the day. Even though we would, again, be badly outnumbered, I came up with a plan to defeat them.

My plan was inspired by a technique that local country people used to hunt for mice in rice fields. Rice field mice were bigger than average house mice because, of course, they ate a lot of rice. After the harvest season, these mice would eat whatever was left over from the harvest. They would burrow in holes in the ground, one hole to enter and another hole to exit. The country people would wrap straw in a bundle, light it up and place it in a hole. The smoke would force the mice to scurry out of another hole. With the mice out of the ground, the country people could then easily hunt them for food. If this worked to expose mice, why would it not work on enemy soldiers? I briefed my first commander, General Thonglid, and my second commander, General Chao Wannasang, about my plan. They were not the least bit interested in my plan. In fact, they thought I was crazy. They even yelled at me for suggesting such a ridiculous strategy. Killing mice was one thing, but this was the ruthless and vicious NVA we were talking about. There was no way of knowing if this plan could work on the enemy because my commanders had never heard of anything like this being used in combat. I argued with them. "I only have 250 men," I said. "To go up against 2,000 to 3,000 NVA this way, while they are in one place with only one way out, is worth the risk and it will keep my men safe and alive." These generals continued to argue with me and sneered, "If your crazy plan does not work, how safe and alive will you all be then?" I did not have time to think of any other plan, so I made an offer to them. "Use my salary to pay for the plan I am suggesting. If the plan fails, and if I am still alive, then throw me in jail." The generals saw that I was serious and that I was willing to risk everything to win this battle and keep my men safe. The generals finally agreed to give me what I needed to "smoke out" and ambush the enemy.

Helicopters dropped me and 250 troops off in Khammouan. Not too long afterwards, they also dropped off large 50-pound bags of dry chili peppers and firecrackers from our base in Vientiane. These were the key ingredients needed to execute my plan. We marched to the mountain, a journey which took three days. I had most of my men surround the mountain while I took 12 men with to stake out a position near the opening of the cave area. The NVA was not aware of our presence on the top of the mountain; they thought they were safe in the cave. We opened the bags of dry chili peppers, lit the firecrackers, tossed them into the bags and dropped them down into the volcano hole. What the NVA were soon about to discover is that when chili peppers burn, they give off a horrible smell and act like pepper spray. Without gas masks, the NVA would suffocate and experience burning eyes. We knew that despite their great numbers, the NVA did not have sophisticated supplies like gas masks.

Once we dropped the bags of chili pepper and the firecrackers detonated in the bags, the effects were exactly as I had expected. Thousands of NVA troops had no choice but to flee the cave from the only entrance. When they reached the top of the old volcano hole and ran out, blinded, coughing and choking, we were waiting, fully armed with machine guns. During this one-sided battle, we did not lose any men. It was one of the worst defeats suffered by the NVA. The enemy was baffled for years to come about who came up with such a "crazy" plan. While thousands of NVA died during this ambush, I had to remind myself that in the war zone, it was still, and always would be, kill or be killed. General Thonglid and

General Chao Wannasang certainly had a change of heart in their attitudes towards me. I was promised a promotion, a money reward, and a medal for my heroic actions. Those spoils of victory would have to wait, however, because I was still needed on the battlefield.

CHAPTER EIGHT

I took my troops back to Khammouan in the late summer of 1968. At first, I thought we could rest for a few days. It was not to be. Only two hours after our arrival, I received urgent orders to assist General Vang Pao who had just been beaten by the NVA. General Pao and his Hmong soldiers were stationed at a mountain base called Phou Kood. There were about 200 Lao soldiers up there. There was also a Thai military group of 1000 soldiers called the Black Panther Corps, also known as the BPC, who were supposed to help General Pao. I recall thinking that these Thai soldiers were not experienced, they had limited training, they were unfamiliar with the mountainous territory and, most concerning, they did not understand mindset of the NVA. These Thai soldiers also had supplies and guns from the U.S., and apparently each of them was paid $10,000. Furthermore, their families would receive an additional $10,000 if a Thai soldier was killed. General Pao was recruiting every man who could point and shoot a gun. The reality was that no amount of money was going to win a war without quality soldiers.

There was speculation that the BPC was a group recruited by the CIA to assist Laos fight the NVA. The reason that was suspected was because there was a reasonable fear by the U.S. that the NVA, and by extension, communism, would spread down to Thailand. Another reason had to do with everything I had noticed and learned about how these Thai soldiers were armed, supplied and paid. During the summer of 1968, I did not know much about the CIA or about any of its possible activities in Thailand. At that time, I did not think the CIA was helping the BPC. On the contrary, I believed that the government of Thailand was sending in the troops to help support Laos to stop the NVA from landing in Thailand. Today, with hindsight, there is a strong belief that the CIA was behind the BPC. The reason for this belief is that Thai soldiers had previously never helped Laos in military combat. A Thai documentary suggested that the CIA indeed went into Thailand. Its purpose was to recruit good men for the military to help train undocumented Hmong Thai men to fight communists. These men were secretly released from the Thai military so they would receive double pay, which was partially paid for by the CIA. These men were trained only for three to six months, and then they were stationed at Phou Kood. Their names were those later identified as being members of the BPC.

I recall the first time I met General Vang Pao after the helicopter dropped me off at the base up on Phou Kood. My father knew General Vang Pao well. He lived on a big compound in u-shaped three-story brick house with one Lao wife, 16 Hmong wives and many children. It was a Hmong custom for men to have more than one wife. The compound was also designed so a helicopter could land on the roof. General Vang Pao also had a military meeting room on the second floor where he could meet with officers of the rank Captain and above.

When we arrived at Phou Kood, I lined up my men and then talked to General Vang Pao. I informed General Vang Pao that my men had never been in this area before so I needed one of his men to work with us because they know the area better. Without a second thought, General Vang Pao insisted that I use all 200 of his men. No sooner than he gave me all of his soldiers, General Vang Pao just left.

I learned from our spies that there would be at least 10,000 NVA troops on Phou Bia, the tallest mountain in Laos. A communication radar station was set up on that mountain. The NVA controlled that mountain which enabled them to get clear shots at the U.S. airplanes with their Soviet-made anti-aircraft guns. These guns were actually four guns together. One soldier would turn the gun while three soldiers would shoot. The result was a "death zone" to prevent the U.S. from delivering supplies to Laos as well to provide aerial support bombings. The NVA stronghold on the mountain area also prevented delivery supplies by foot.

When we launched an offensive on Phou Bia, the NVA responded by shooting at us day and night. We suffered significant casualties. The terrain did not help our situation. One side was hilly and surrounded by NVA. The other side was a cliff, and at the bottom of the cliff, we were also surrounded by NVA. We had no choice but to risk our lives and climb down with a rope on the cliff side. It was very dangerous. It did not help that we were also running out of food, guns, supplies and ammunition. Of the 355 men I started out with, I was now only fighting with 85 men. Where I could once call in for air support from F-16 airplanes, that option was no longer available because of the NVA fortification on the mountain armed with big anti-aircraft guns. We needed help and we needed it right away.

I made the difficult decision to take 12 other men with me from the battlefield and take the seven-day journey to the capital of Luang Prabang. When we finally arrived in the city, we went straight to the military base there. I anticipated the meeting I was about to have was going to be contentious so I came up with a strategy before I entered the room. I told my men if they heard any gunshots, enter the room, and kill everybody in there. I also told them if something happened to me and they had to kill the people in that room, to make sure to escape from the base. I gave this order because the General and Colonel I was about to meet with were known for their hair trigger tempers and violent tendencies.

My men and I were then taken to the commander room where we met with General/Prince Vanna Sang. I explained to the General the status of the battle, and how we were at a disadvantage because of a severe shortage of supplies and support. I was told that Colonel Keo was in charge of sending supplies to us so there should be no problem. "If there is no problem," I shot back, "why did we take such a risk and leave the battlefield to come here to ask for help?" General Vanna Sang saw how serious I was. He radioed Colonel Keo to come into the commander room right away. When Colonel Keo arrived and learned about what this meeting was about, he was furious that I jumped the chain of command by going to the General before going to him. Colonel Keo defended himself by saying that planes could not drop off supplies into that "death zone." I asked him why they could not have delivered the supplies by foot? Colonel Keo told me that he was not given that order by General Vanna Sang. Now the General lost his temper. He yelled back at Colonel Keo that he did indeed give him those orders.

General Vanna Sang then pulled out his pistol and slammed it onto his big desk, a definite sign that he was upset at Colonel Keo for failing to deliver supplies to my base. Precious time was being wasted and by now I was mad at both of them because they were blaming each other. I pulled out my sidearm pistol and slammed on his desk to show that I was ready to do anything right now to get supplies to my men. General Vanna Sang and Colonel Keo were taken aback by my action. General Vanna Sang demanded to know if I had come to kill him. I yelled back at him and said, "Yes, I will if you do not help our soldiers right now who put their lives in jeopardy for the country!" At this point, because of all of the commotion, my 12 men ran in to the commander room and pointed their guns at Colonel Keo and General Vanna Sang. These commanding officers were really shocked now. They seemed to calm down at once. General Vanna Sang finally gave Colonel

Keo the clear and unmistakable order to send all the supplies and men that I needed immediately. I gave a hand signal for my men to put down their guns.

This was a big story and there was much talk among the military leaders in Laos that I had stood up to General Vanna Sang and Colonel Keo. I had no choice in the matter. If I had not alerted them, the military personnel in the capital would never have known the sense of urgency of the situation at Phou Kood. However, that was not the end of my face off with General Vanna Sang. He called my father, who was also a general, and complained that I almost killed him. An exaggerated account by General Vanna Sang, of course, but it caused my father to meet with me at the military base. After I gave my father the accurate account of what really happened, he told me that I did the right thing. All I was trying to do was protect and speak up for my men who were fighting for a unified cause. My father then confronted General Vanna Sang and told him that I did the right thing, that I was a patriot and was willing to fight for my men. He also told the General, "If you can't support our men by air you have to support them by ground. You can't jeopardize the troops like that." In no time, despite the risks, U.S.-supplied T-28 bombers were sent to clear the area for the supply drop. Food, ammunition, and medical supplies were loaded into a helicopter to send to the Phou Kood base. Mission accomplished.

CHAPTER NINE

Phou Kood was the last battle I fought in for a while. I was informed that there was a U.S.-backed fund set up with the purpose of sending qualified Laotian men to pursue continued legal training for the military. I was qualified because I already had earned a law degree, and I had military training. To my surprise, no one in the higher ranks tried to talk me into staying on the battlefield; rather, they wanted me to continue my legal education. Perhaps General Vanna Sang and Colonel Keo did not want me to be in a position to pay them another visit!

In order for me to be admitted into this advanced legal program, I had to pass a difficult test. The test subjects included military law, math, English, and French. I took a test preparation class for the test because I had been away fighting for so long, and I certainly needed to brush up on these subjects. I sat for the exam with 400 other men and then waited for the results.

While I waited for the results of the legal exam, I stayed home with my family and spent time with my girlfriend, Kelly Insixiangmai. Kelly was my first true love. We met back in high school but we only spoke to each other after school. We would go out to the street vendors after school, get something to eat and walk along the scenic Mekong River. Sometimes I took her to the movies. Kelly's father, Leum Insixiangmai, was a mayor of Vientiane. Her family was considered very upper class. Whoever wanted to date the mayor's daughter, that person had to either be in the same class, wealthier, or have a high rank in the military. Kelly and I would sneak out to see each other when we started dating. I did not introduce myself to Kelly's family until years later when I was close to completing my law school/military training program. One of the reasons for this delay was that during high school, we were expected to concentrate on our studies, not dating. It was a cultural custom that I was expected to observe, even though for one of the rare times in my life I broke the rules.

When I first arrived at Kelly's family home, I was dressed in my military uniform. I walked straight up to her parents first, paid my respects, and introduced myself. I made sure to mention who my parents were, and that my father was a high-ranking military officer. Kelly's father then asked, "What are you here for?" I replied that I liked his daughter and I wanted to ask her out to the movies. Mayor Insixiangmai said, "OK, you can go to the movies, but Kelly has to take her older brother with her."

Respecting his wishes, we went to the movies with Kelly's older brother Keophet on our first "official date." Mayor Insixiangmai knew who my parents were so that is why he allowed Kelly and me to go out. However, for the first six or seven dates, we had to be chaperoned by Kelly's older brother.

Once Kelly's parents and my parents saw that things were serious between us, my father and mother invited her parents to their house for dinner. The families knew of each other, but it was the first time they had dined together. My family wanted to know what kind of girl Kelly was. My father certainly approved of Kelly. Who could not approve of her? She was lovely, pretty, soft spoken, she liked to cook, and she would be a good wife. Most importantly, my family wanted to make sure that she cared for me. This was all leading up to make it official that Kelly and I were boyfriend and girlfriend. That way, I could visit her any time now. After a few months of dating, my parents gave Kelly a generous gift worth 500,000 kip which represented a "promise" for our relationship. It was a proud moment when, after I finished my military training, I dressed up in my uniform, rode my motorcycle up to Kelly's house and took her out to celebrate our future together.

I received additional good news when I was accepted to the advanced legal training program six days after taking the entrance exam. I was one of 47 men who were accepted to the two-year program at the National University of Singapore. Kelly and I discussed it, decided we would wait for me to finish my schooling in Singapore, and then we would get engaged.

I arrived at the National University of Singapore in late 1968. I lived on the military base, and a military bus picked me up each morning to take me to the law school. The program consisted of a combination of advanced legal training and participating in real trials. The biggest case I worked on involved a soldier who was selling drugs and was involved with the murder of a civilian. The defendant was selling heroin and ordered the murder of the entire civilian family who owed the drug dealer money. We had solid proof that the defendant ordered the murder of the family because we found the man who received the order to kill the family. We found this man because one person survived the attack, and they recalled what he looked like. Three men actually came to kill the family with guns. One family member survived and remembered the face of one of the killers. However, the three assassins had an associate who threatened the surviving family member; if he testified against the assassins, they would kill him. The surviving family member was not going to be silenced. He told us that he was not afraid to testify because he had nothing left to lose. To ensure this man's safety, we also provided witness protection to him. This was a very difficult case for me to work on. I worked with the investigator of the case, was given the responsibility to address the court at times and the whole case overall was very challenging. However, I had seen such horrors on the battlefield that I could stomach the gruesome facts of a murder case and the bloody and violent crime scene while staying focused on the prosecution against these violent men. The great news was that we won the case; it ended in a victory for my team. The men were convicted. In addition, the victims' family was also awarded monetary damages.

I graduated my advanced legal program in middle of 1970. I returned to Vientiane on a 747 plane, dressed was in full white military uniform. When I disembarked from the plane, there was a welcome home ceremony at the airport. My plan was to get engaged to Kelly. However, life did not go according to plan. When I came back from Singapore, conditions in Laos were growing more chaotic by the day. Communist efforts to spread down into Laos had intensified, and our country was becoming more and more unstable. My father was out on the frontlines more often. Kelly's father had to deal with the political crises since he was the mayor of Vientiane. Everyone seemed to be getting pulled in different directions and were distracted. I was not spared by the chaos, especially when it came to my involvement in the arrest of Uncle Ouane.

Everyone in the family basically got along with Uncle Ouane, and I was his favorite nephew. Yet no one in our family, my grandfather and father especially, liked that Uncle Ouane was involved the drug trade. Unfortunately, there was nothing anybody could do to stop it. He was in control of heroin factories and had protected the opium trade for years. Time and again, Uncle Ouane was advised by everyone not to be involved in drugs. Time and again, Uncle Ouane boasted, "No one can stop me." Uncle Ouane had every right to be confident of his power. An ally of the United States during the Vietnam War, Uncle Ouane developed a close relationship with William H Sullivan, the U.S. Ambassador to Laos, and Ted Shackley, the CIA station chief in Vientiane. Despite the intense conflicts amongst the Forces Armees du Royaume (FAR)regional commanders,

Uncle Ouane was pivotal in providing loyal military support against the NVA and the Pathet Lao in the northern regions of Laos. Previous attempts to arrest Uncle Ouane had all failed. Uncle Ouane paid off anyone who tried to stop his drug trafficking operation, and to make matters worse, those men who were paid off were then arrested for bribery and imprisoned for life.

How was it, then, that I was picked to arrest my own relative? The Prime Minister of Laos, Chao Souvanna Phouma, ordered the operation to arrest Uncle Ouane. He wanted to get rid of corrupt and illegal officials in the government and in the military. Historically, the government refused to pick a relative to go after another relative because it was considered a conflict of interest. In this case, the military men looked carefully at Uncle Ouane's background, they looked at my background, and found out that Uncle Ouane was not blood related. I was finally told by the military about the mission to arrest Uncle Ouane. They told me the U.S. was aware that Uncle Ouane had a monopoly on the Laos heroin trade. Uncle Ouane had also caused considerable embarrassment to the U.S. Embassy by using Laotian Air Force T-28 fighters to attack an opium convoy near Nam Keung. He then boasted, "I was entrusted by the Government to make sure the army got its share of the opium trade." Laos had no drug laws so the U.S. feared that pressuring Uncle Ouane to get out of the narcotics business might somehow damage the war effort. There was also the concern that many soldiers in Vietnam were becoming addicted to heroin processed in labs protected by those who worked for Uncle Ouane. However, pressuring the Lao government to act was another matter. The U.S. Ambassador to Laos, G. McMurtrie Godley, was quoted as saying, "I believe the Royal Laotian Government takes its responsibility seriously to prohibit international opium traffic."

After providing me with all this information, the military men at this meeting wanted to know if I was willing to carry out the mission to arrest Uncle Ouane. Without hesitation, I told them I was accepting the mission. I recalled the promise I made my grandfather many years ago that I would be the one to defeat Uncle Ouane. I spoke to my father before the raid and let him know what was going to happen. My father pointed out to me that if Uncle Ouane did not love his country, I should do what I have to do and take care of the problem. Grandpa had taught my father and I that it does not matter what country you are from (Grandpa, for example, was not born a Lao citizen), you protect the country you are at, obey its laws and be honest.

Armed with a court order, dressed in my full military outfit, and accompanied by a group of nine soldiers for backup, I headed to Uncle Ouane's large house in Luang Prabang. I knew the way well because Uncle Ouane's house was located not far from Grandpa's house. Once we arrived, I gave my men the order to stand guard outside the house. My blood ran hot at that moment because it would not have surprised me if Uncle Ouane tried to kill me. I already knew the exact layout of the house, having been there many times before as a young boy. After making sure my radio was turned on so I could communicate with my men, I walked into the house alone and headed right down into the basement. Uncle Ouane's guards stopped me before I entered the basement. I made sure these guards could see my radio and warned them that my guards would blow up the whole house if anything happened to me. With that understanding, the guards lowered their guns and let me enter the basement.

The basement where Uncle Ouane's opium operations took place was very large, probably close to 2600 square feet. In addition to the many armed guards, there were 17 or 18 people working down there around the clock making opium. Uncle Ouane approached me with a grin and announced, "Oh, nephew. I knew you were coming. I'm happy to see you." Of course, Uncle Ouane knew I was coming. I was certain that with his influence and power, someone slipped the word to him once I got the court order to arrest him. Uncle Ouane then showed me a suitcase. He opened it up, and it was full of money. He then said, "I gave the guy before you a smaller suitcase so this one is for you. It will take care of you for life." I told Uncle Ouane that no one can buy me. Uncle Ouane was shocked at first, and then he got very mad. He barked at me, "We are related! I am your grandfather's son even though we are not blood related. You should show me some respect!" I said what I was doing now had nothing to do with family; I vowed to do everything to do my duty and protect my country. This seemed to anger Uncle Ouane even more. He called my father, complained that I showed him no respect and that he would never allow me to get promoted. My father said, "My son will not be bribed by you, and I can't make him do anything, he's just doing his job." Uncle Ouane then tried to get the Prime Minister to put me in jail. What Uncle Ouane did not realize was that it was the Prime

Minister who ordered this mission, and he told Uncle Ouane it was him that was going to jail. Uncle Ouane did not know what had just hit him. He surrendered without a fight. I led Uncle Ouane out of his house and took him to a district jail for government officials. That jail was known to be a very tough place. Uncle Ouane was stripped of his military rank, and he was finally behind bars. While I was proud to have carried out my mission, I found it strange that, even though the Prime Minister wanted to get rid of corrupt officials, there was no publicity about the arrest. I was about to find out more about why governments work hard to keep their secrets.

CHAPTER TEN

In 1971, I was privately recognized for arresting Uncle Ouane at an award ceremony. The ceremony took place at a hall at a military base in Vientiane by the Congress house. My parents were in attendance as the Prime Minister gave me an award. After I accepted the award, I walked past four American men. They all shook my hand, congratulated me on what I had done, and introduced themselves as working for the Central Intelligence Agency and Air America. They said they would like to talk to me some more at a later time. I thanked them and then left to celebrate with my family.

I did not give that brief introduction another thought during the next two months. During that time, I was both student and teacher as I was involved in more military training on the base. The higher ranked commanders who were still out in the field were educating and updating us on how to fight the NVA. I also oversaw training the Hmong military about how we could protect our country from communism and stop the NVA from coming into Laos.

I was so busy that life got in the way again, and Kelly and I postponed our engagement. I was off doing my military training and my father, who was in charge of the wedding ceremony plans, was away fighting for long periods of time. There was still so much instability in the country in general that it was an inconvenience for everyone to discuss, let alone plan, a wedding. Kelly and I discussed it and agreed that when everything calmed down then we would get married.

A couple of months after the award ceremony, my commanding officer summoned me for a meeting. I was informed that the Vice Prime Minister of Laos, Colonel Insisiangmay, was also representing the CIA in Laos. I learned that earlier that year, the Prime Minister and King of Laos traveled to the U.S. to ask for help against the NVA and China. That help turned out to be CIA training in Laos. Colonel Insisiangmay now needed men ranked captain and above in Laos to be trained by the CIA and to fight against the communists. It was clear to me that my commander was aware that my father had previously worked with the CIA. I was then informed I had to pass some tests to be officially selected.

At the time, I certainly wanted to be part of the CIA. I had seen enough to realize that without help from the U.S., Laos would be very vulnerable. The fight against the NVA would be less successful without the U.S. it would take more than just our will power and manpower. I also believed that the more advanced training from the CIA would provide our country with more tools to help defeat the NVA.

I was given a test preparation booklet to study for the test. While the test was going to be given in my native Laotian language, I had to know some basic English because if I was selected, I would need to be able to communicate with Americans. Fortunately, I had a working knowledge of English because in high school I attended an *English As A Second Language* class. Other subjects that were on the test were math and French.

The first part of this written test was administered on the military base in Vientiane and it was about three or four hours long. In addition to the multiple-choice questions that tested basic subjects, there was a psychological part of the test that required written answers. There was a question about if you were surrounded by the enemy what would you do? Since I had been a military leader, I could easily answer that one. I would get out as best as I could, arrange for support, and try to lose as few men as possible. I used my experience in the battle of Phou Kood as an example. We were on top of the mountain, being bombarded and slaughtered, with a severe lack of supplies. I knew if I stayed there, the rest of my men would die, so I had to leave to try to get some help. That was why I took the risk, climbed down the cliff and went back to the base for help.

Another question I recall being asked was if you were captured by the enemy and interrogated, what would you do? The question went on to ask if the enemy said, "If you tell us the truth, we will let you go," what would you do? Would you believe them? I answered that I would always assume that the enemy would never let me go, that they would kill me even if I told them everything. I also would never tell the enemy who I worked for, or what my mission was. I would always lie to the enemy if I knew I was going to die in the end anyway. If I was ever asked who I worked for, I would only answer that I served the Royal Lao Army. I would never admit that I worked for the CIA.

The last example of a psychological question I was asked was about how I would spy on the enemy. What would my technique be to infiltrate the enemy territory and gather intelligence? I had experience in this area as well from my time on the battlefield. I answered that I would remove my uniform and make myself look more like a local civilian. I would then do what the locals do, and blend into the daily activities in the area to try to get info from the people and earn the trust of the locals to get information about the enemy.

A week later, the results were posted on a list on the military base. Out of the 100 men who took this first test, 50 passed, and I was one of them. For those of us who passed the first written test, we were then subjected to a physical test and a medical exam. The medical exam was done to make sure one was not disabled or physically limited in any way. The physical test required us to do push-ups, run, lift weights and jump as high as we could. All 50 of us passed this part of the test.

The last part of the test would determine who would be admitted into the CIA training class. All 50 of us were led into a big room that had a window, one door and two tall gas tanks. A plainclothes CIA officer, speaking in English, and using an interpreter to speak to us in Laotian, gave us the following instructions: "We are going to release gas into this room. This is something that the enemy could do to you if they capture you. We need to see how long you can hold your breath. Unlike the enemy, we will not allow you to die. We will leave the door unlocked. You can leave the room any time you want."

The CIA officer turned off the lights in the room, turned on the gas, and he and the interpreter left the room.

It did not take long for me to smell the fumes, which smelled like cooking gas. The room was dark so I could not see how the other men were reacting at first. It did not matter if it was dark because soon, I could not open my eyes anyway; they were watering and my nose was running from the gas. What I could not tell was that 29 men ran out of that room. The remaining 21 of us stayed in that room until we all passed out from holding our breath. The short-term pain of that test was worth it. It turned out that whoever could withstand the gas and did not run out of the room were chosen to be in the CIA training class.

After passing all of the tests, I met with four CIA officials at the military base in Vientiane. As was the case before the gas test, the CIA used an interpreter who worked with Air America to help communicate with me. I was informed that I was in the very first CIA training class in Laos. My father had assisted the CIA on an individual basis and had never been trained by them. I was informed that training classes would begin in one week, that the training would last for six months, and that they would take place in Udon, Thailand. The training would take place there because the instructors from the U.S military could not be in Laos but they could be in Thailand. I was also informed that even though I was now a member of the CIA I was also officially still in the Royal Lao Army. That dual association meant that I would be paid twice per month from each organization. The last piece of information I received was that any of 21 men selected in the class could still be kicked out at any time if any of us failed to perform well during the training.

Before I left for Thailand, my father gave me his perspective about me working with the CIA. He said that the U.S. is the most powerful country in the world, and it has the most potential and best capabilities to help the Lao military defeat the NVA and the communist government. His words gave me added confidence about the new journey I was about to embark on.

One week later I gathered with the other 20 Laotian men who had been selected for the first CIA training class. I knew some of the members of my class from my days back at officers' training school. We took a boat across the Mekong River, arrived in Thailand then travelled by military bus to the military base in Udon. Once we arrived at the base, we received a uniform, bedding supplies, pajamas, white t-shirt, boxers, shoes, military uniforms and supplies. It began to feel just like basic training all over again. I would soon find out that basic training was a vacation compared to what I was about to be subjected to.

The CIA training was intense from day one. We woke up early every day. We ran and did vigorous calisthenics. We were instructed how to communicate with the CIA because of the sensitive nature of the information. We were taught how to report intelligence, how to call the headquarters, and how to execute Morse code. We also had to learn many secret codes. The secret codes were specific numbers and words which served several purposes. For example, certain codes revealed directions to where you are located and locations of different military bases. Other codes were also used to send messages ordering aerial support bombing. For example, "red sky" meant an order for aerial bombs, while "339" was also code for a request for bombing. I had to memorize so many codes! Mountains in Laos were assigned codes to differentiate those in the northern, central, and southern parts of the country. When a number for one of them was mentioned, it would indicate what part of the country that mountain was located. We had to study maps of China, as well as maps of North and

South Vietnam. We were debriefed by CIA officers who were spies. They reported to us in detail what they had learned from infiltrating the NVA. One Laotian instructor who had infiltrated the communist ranks described to us how he blended in with the villagers, acted like he was one of them and absorbed their ways of doing things. This agent's cover was a typical village farmer, and he acted like a quiet, uneducated person. He learned how to read the map of Laos, and discovered how many provinces, districts, and areas were heavily populated by the NVA. We learned how the NVA lived in certain villages and caves. We received training on how communists thought and compiled a complete psychological profile of the NVA. The NVA were typically trained from a young age to hate Americans. They were indoctrinated with the belief that that Americans would not hesitate to kill them so that that they would grow to hate the U.S. and anyone associated with the U.S. The crucial part of any NVA psychological profile was that they would never, ever, tell the truth. There was no mistaking this fact that communists would always lie about everything. Their entire history was all made up, and there is, and never has been, any truth in their story. They would do anything to get the result they were aiming for. I had seen this play out during my time in the battlefield. For example, if the NVA wanted to get into a village, they would do and say anything to gain trust to make the villagers believe that they were good and would bring peace. However, if one did not volunteer to fight for the communist cause, they would immediately be branded an enemy, and that person would be eliminated.

Interrogation training was also another intense part of our training. Not only were we taught how to interrogate others, but we were trained how to handle being interrogated. If I was able to interrogate someone, I was taught how to first ask the basic questions: name, where the enemy was from, and their intentions – were they forced to come here or did they come willingly to Laos? I was taught to always be prepared for rough interrogations. I was to assume that kind and polite requests often did not work so sometimes force was needed forceful to get information. We had to quickly size up the interrogation subject's personality because some people were easier than others to get information from. During our training, especially when we were the subjects of the interrogation, instructors did not hit us but they told us that when real interrogations happened, the enemy would hit us with their fist, a gun or subject us to electric shocks. No matter what force we were subjected to, we were told in no uncertain terms to not give the NVA the truth no matter what. On the other hand, we were told to physically force the NVA to give up information if they resisted. We had to do whatever was necessary to get information. If all else failed, and if there were many interrogation subjects in the room, we had to sacrifice one to show the others we meant business. We were taught how to spot when an interrogation subject was lying. When we were asking questions, if the subject moved around, looked away to the left, and avoided eye contact then it was likely the subject was lying. When we had to lie under interrogation, we had to convince ourselves to believe in what we were telling our captors and stick to that story. The CIA spent about three weeks with us on this part of training.

An offshoot of our interrogation training was taught by an American instructor. The topic was how to beat a lie detector test. I was taught to control my heart rate and my emotions in the event I was taken prisoner by the enemy. I was also taught to do this to make the test show I was telling the truth. Sensors from a polygraph machine were connected to my body and around my right arm. The instructor would ask me all sorts of questions and I would have to answer in ways to show how my heartbeat and emotions affected the polygraph read-out. I then would lie in my answers to show that there was no change in my heartbeat and that the polygraph would not show that I was lying.

We learned how to use different kinds of weapons and ammunition, including the M16, AK47, .45, M14, M40, M38., Soviet-made guns and American-made guns. We had to be able to take any gun apart and put them back together... while blindfolded! When we picked up one piece of a gun, we had to know which piece belonged to what gun, then find another piece, then find the proper bullet for that gun and then shoot it. I prepared so well, and I was so familiar with the types of guns that when I touched a piece of a gun, I immediately knew what kind it was. The purpose of the exercise for blindly identifying guns was that during times when we would be in the dark, if we ran out of bullets and reached out for guns from dead bodies, we would need to know how to use that weapon. Also, it was important for us to know how to fix guns if they got stuck, and how to clean any type of gun.

Another part of our training was something I was already familiar with; how to dismantle bombs. We learned about different types of bombs, from land mines to grenades. We learned about the ways to use these bombs and ways to disarm them.

While I also had a solid background in the basics of treating wounds, I received more advanced training in treating injuries from gunshots, bomb blasts and burns. I was taught to identify different kinds of wounds, which guns and weapons caused the wound and what kind of medicines to use. I was also trained how to deal with someone when they were badly wounded. I had seen plenty of instances during the war where someone was badly wounded. Many times, they would cry, scream, and express their fear of dying. I was taught how to talk to them, how to calm them down, and, if it was appropriate in the situation, to reference people that were hurt worse who ended up recovering. In instances where the injury was fatal, we were reminded to assure the wounded person that we would be there with him until the end. These lessons also helped prepare us for a time if we were injured. During these times, it was very easy to get shot, to lose a limb and to die. It was important to know how to treat yourself if you were injured. I was able to share with my instructors some information I learned out in the field. For example, I told them that the enemy used bullets which were laced with a toxic chemical at the tip. If the bullet was stuck in the body for a long period of time it would paralyze the victim. It was important for our troops to know that if a soldier was shot with these bullets, they had to be removed from the body immediately. Grandpa would have been proud to know I was being trained in these medical procedures.

We were taught the complex psychology of how to talk to, and deal with, our military superiors, peers and those officers serving below us. The horrors of war are real and we, as well as our troops, had to prepare for those horrors. We were given advice to prepare for dangerous situations and missions. For example, when leading a 12-man team going into a danger zone or a village, the leader must go forward to check out the place is safe for the rest of the platoon to follow. If all is safe, he will signal the team, take the team, and walk forward. Another example involved a situation where troops were on top of a mountain and planning to move to the next mountain. We were instructed to stay in position for at least two nights, check on the next mountain we were going to move to, and make sure there were no NVA soldiers staked out there. Tactics we were taught to employ included using a telescope to check to make sure bushes do not suddenly appear where there were none before, and to make sure there were no changes in the terrain or landscape.

Survival skills were part of our training. Sometimes in the jungle the only thing one could find to eat were snakes. If Laos was known as the land of a million elephants, the Laos jungles are known as the land of a million snakes. We were taught to skin the snake, extract the snake meat, and cut it into small pieces. It was obviously very important to cut the snake's neck off to make sure we did not ingest any of its venom. The same technique was to be used for raccoons, squirrels, and any other animals we could find. Of course, because I had taken a vow to follow the Five Precepts, I had to pray to my Buddha Master for permission to eat those taboo creatures to survive. We were also taught how to identify which plants were safe to eat and which were not.

Our training in survival skills also included being flown in a helicopter over a body of water, then being kicked, or pushed out of the helicopter We were given five days to get from that drop location to another designated location. We were in full uniform and gear when we landed in the water, and we could easily drown with all the weight of our gear. Once we swam to the shore, we walked through the jungle and up a mountain. All we had was a map and a bit of canned food. We were left to find our own way to the destination. Once we reached the location on the map, we lit a smoke signal so a helicopter would pick us up.

During our training, we did get intelligence briefings about the ongoing Vietnam War. The fighting had become very heavy in Vietnam, Laos, and Cambodia. It was drummed into us that the dangers we would face had increased and intensified. Each day of the war made conditions more dangerous than before. We were warned that we had to be more careful than ever when venturing into villages because the NVA could be more mixed in and hidden among the locals. I knew I would not just be facing communists but also political people in Laos who were naïve about the communist system. I recall that knowing some of our political leaders were not well educated about communism became a nagging worry of mine.

By the end of 1971, after six months of training with no breaks, I was among the 21-man inaugural graduating Lao class trained by the CIA. There was hardly any time for rest or self-congratulations. Duty called practically right away.

CHAPTER ELEVEN

After a very brief break from my six-month CIA training, I returned to the military base in Vientiane. Our 21-man CIA team met with the Prime Minister and Vice Prime Minister. We all received our training completion certificates and our per diem money. Then it was back to business, and we were given our assignments. There were five areas in Laos where we could possibly be assigned to: 1) Luang Prabang, 2) Long Chang (where General Vang Pao was and where Hmong people lived), 3) Savanakhet, 4) Paksey and 5) Vientiane, the new capital. I was assigned to patrol Savanahket and Paksey, which was considered a plum, albeit dangerous, assignment. The reason for the danger was that those areas were linked by mountains and forests, and they were also close to the Ho Chi Minh trail.

Me and my 12-man team, who were also part of the CIA training class, were transported and dropped off at a mountain called Phou Salao. We went to the higher part of the mountain so we could see the Ho Chi Minh trail coming from North Vietnam. On this day, we saw 17 cargo trucks loaded with NVA soldiers. I noticed most of them stood up in the truck. I assumed that was because they always wanted to be ready for action. Branches were placed on top of the trucks, and in front of the trucks. The NVA soldiers even put branches over their heads as camouflage. Some of the soldiers were sitting in front of the trucks, some of them were walking, and some were using bicycles to carry food supplies. One truck was dragging an anti-aircraft machine gun. The transport was moving very fast, and we did not detect that any of the NVA were talking. This was an urgent development, so I immediately called the military base in Udon, Thailand. My CIA liaison in Udon was a Laotian-to-English interpreter named Colonel Nook. Colonel Nook answered my call personally. I explained to him what was happening at that moment on the Ho Chi Minh trail and requested an air strike. Colonel Nook agreed with my assessment of the situation. He relayed the orders for an air strike. Soon enough, four incoming F-16's roared overhead. The fighter jets swooped in as low as possible and bombed the entire transport. Following the successful attack, my men and I climbed down the mountain and counted the number of the dead. We had prevented more than 1,000 NVA from accomplishing their mission. But we knew that was a temporary setback for them. They would soon have another 1,000-man transport on the way.

We then moved up north on foot, staying clear of directly walking along the Ho Chi Minh trail. We stuck to traveling in the deep forest and taking advantage of the cover provided by the big trees. One challenge of traveling off the beaten path was that we encountered leeches. They would lay in wait as soon as someone walked by, then they would jump on the body. They also dropped from the trees. Those leeches would get into our shoes or on our body and then they would suck our blood until they grew very large. Most of the jungles in Laos had leeches all over the place. I was somewhat used to leeches because they also lived in the rice fields in Laos. The only remedy to keep them away was to rub diesel oil on our faces and body because the leeches were repelled by that odor.

While we were making our way through the dense and leech-filled jungle, we heard the movements of the NVA. All 12 of us spread out and buried ourselves in the ground. We covered ourselves with leaves, leaving spaces for our eyes and nose. One of my men got stepped on by an NVA soldier. The NVA soldier yelled out that he stepped on someone. We wasted no time and stated shooting. A battle broke out, 32 NVA soldiers against the 12 of us. We lost five men during the battle but ended up killing all 32 NVA soldiers. We hurried to a safe area and radioed for a helicopter to get us out of there. While we waited, we quickly buried the five men we lost because there was no time to bring them to the helicopter.

As soon as I came back from the Ho Chi Minh trail, I was ordered to the Luang Prabang area. I was reunited with my old friend Bounchanh during this time. Bounchanh was also involved with a different group supported by the CIA. It was during a time when the NVA were entering the northern part of Laos across the King's rice fields, around 20 kilometers from Luang Prabang palace. There were a lot of mountains in the area. I was fighting on the mountain called Cuekachum. I was east of the Pakou River near the mountain, and Bounchanh was fighting on the west side. The military code for the mountain was "787." Our mission was to drive the NVA and the Lao communists off the mountain. General Chao Sinh Saysana, who descended from the Royal Family of Laos, was our commanding officer. I led Battalion 112, Bounchanh led Battalion 114 and Battalion 15 was led by Colonel Do.

While I was stationed at Cuekachum, me and my troops were surrounded by the NVA. We were, as usual, badly outnumbered. Out of the 400 men I had arrived with, 200 had been killed, while the NVA had 5,000 to 6,000 troops. Everywhere I looked, there were dead soldiers on land and floating in the river. I radioed for support. Even though my friend Bounchanh was not in any better of a situation (out of the 175 men he arrived with, he had lost 50 men), he answered my call. Bounchanh had also gotten the word that a NVA caravan with guns, food, and ammunition was headed towards the Namseung River. Bounchanh ordered his communication men to contact the U.S. forces in Thailand to drop bombs from B-52 to rescue me and my troops. This was known as a big battle called Phou Soy 787.

In 1972, following the Battle of Phou Soy 787, Bounchanh and I were ordered to help General Vang Pao and the Hmong military in Long Chang. Bounchanh was with a U.S. solider named Mr. Lay who was part of Battalion BA110. Mr. Lay was also a commander who was ordered to bring men in to assist General Vang Pao. Mr. Lay was standing close to an airplane that was attacked by the NVA The plane exploded and the huge blast killed Mr. Lay.

When we had a break for some R & R in Vientiane, I would go out with Bounchanh. We would go to the social club at the Ponekhemg military base. They had a bar with live bands playing. Bounchanh was more outgoing than me. He was a good dancer, enjoyed his beer and whiskey, smoked cigarettes and was known as a playboy. He had a different girlfriend for every different night we went out. A lot of ladies liked Bounchanh, that was for sure. I was much quieter and more reserved, I did not smoke or carouse, and I only drank orange juice. I did not drink as part of my observance of the Five Precepts. Bounchanh would make fun of me for not having all the girlfriends he had. Bounchanh also always seemed to have more money in his pocket than I did. When we went out in the city, Bounchanh would always give me money to spend. However, it was always Bounchanh who would get the girls. When we went out, because we were captains, we could carry concealed weapons. One time, we went out to a local bar and restaurant. There were some teenagers at a nearby table who were drinking and making a lot of noise. Bounchanh called out to them, "Hey brothers, if you're drunk then you better be prepared to go home." These young people looked at Bounchanh. They thought he was just a regular guy and made some rude comments back to him. Bounchanh said, "You know, if you don't listen to me, pretty soon your table is going to be flipped." Bounchanh told me, "Watch, I'm going to teach these kids a lesson." Bounchanh went to the restroom. When he came back out, instead of tucking his gun under his clothing, he made sure he tucked the gun outside his clothing so the kids could see the gun. When the kids saw that Bounchanh was armed, they suddenly became very quiet and ran out of the place very quickly. We had a good laugh over that. Eventually, Bounchanh went to southern Laos, and I went to the north to continue fighting. We would not see each other again for a very long time.

I kept in touch with Kelly even though I was busy with so many military missions. We would write each other letters once or twice a month and they would be delivered by personnel through the military base. I thought of Kelly often but my duty to protect the country came first. If there was no country, our potential future together would be much more difficult to have.

During these times on the battlefield from 1971 to 1972, I was always communicating with Colonel Nook and the CIA about what was happening. Sometimes I would call Colonel Nook or Colonel Nook would relay information to me directly from the CIA. For example, if I saw suspicious activity by the NVA, I would report that to headquarters. Speaking of NVA activity, the frequency of fighting started to slow down. On January 27, 1973, a significant development took place which explained why fighting had died down recently. The U.S. and the NVA signed a treaty at the Majestic Hotel in Paris, formally ending U.S participation in the Vietnam War. A month later, on February 21, 1973 in Vientiane, Laos signed another cease fire with the NVA. A coalition government was to be formed composed of both left and right factions, and to be presided over by Prince Souphanouvong. Coincidentally, Souphanouvong had a Vietnamese wife. The cease fire agreement also outlined 18 rules, also known as an 18-point political program, that had to be followed. Twelve points dealt with domestic politics and six points covered foreign policy and relations. On July 11, 1974, the Third Coalition Government approved the 18-point program. In domestic policies, the political program included the unity of all nationalities in Laos, guaranteed equal rights in the political, economic, cultural and social fields, democratic rights, individual rights and freedom, freedom of religion, freedom of speech, freedom of the press, freedom of assembly, freedom to form political parties and organizations, freedom to vote and freedom to run for election and office, freedom of movement, freedom of residence, freedom of enterprise and rights of private ownership.

Consequently, these principles included human rights for the people. In foreign policy, the six points contained that the U.S., Thailand, and other foreign countries would pull out of Laos.

In 1973, after being in Vientiane for a couple of months, I was assigned to travel to the Philippines for advanced CIA training which was scheduled to last about a year and a half. Only five men were selected for this program. We were considered the best of the best. We were stationed at the University of Philippines, Manila. Our training would be divided up between classes at the university and the military base. Officers would transport me and the other four officers back and forth to school and military training. It was also arranged that we would all be paid in two ways, once by Kingdom of Laos and additional pay by the U.S. military. My salaries were given to my mother every month and I would only keep my per diem pay. My mother used that money to help support the family.

The advanced CIA training took place in the Philippines for three reasons. The first reason was because the country had all the resources and equipment that was required for the training. The training would be like what SEAL training required, and the Philippines had a good location, tools, equipment, ammunition, guns, and all kinds of things similar to what were used in the U.S. The second reason was that the country reflected reality. Filipinos were fighting the communists, and the communists had won over their tribal people in the jungle by brainwashing them. Finally, the Filipino people spoke English well, and they could easily coordinate with the CIA.

We had CIA instructors who were experts in the fields, and they were from the U.S. and the Philippines. One of the objectives of the training was to gain a better understanding of the communist system in the unfortunate event it ever was forced upon Laos, Vietnam, Cambodia, and Thailand. These countries were monarchies, so they were vulnerable to communist destruction of the existing system. We were taught the techniques the communists would use to brainwash the poor, uneducated tribal people, and what they would then do to the big cities. They would wipe out the monarchy and everything would change. They would tell tribal people that because of the current royal government system, that was why they were poor. They would tell them, "If we come in, we will make you rich, whatever you want you will get it. Once we clean out the royal government everything will change and there will be peace." It was a chilling prediction, yet we could see the writing on the wall if communists won the war. Communists would tell us the white lies, but the truth would be black. They meant the opposite of everything they said. I thought back to the fact that the King of Laos had asked Geneva to make it a neutral country back in 1961-1962. After trying to avoid the conflict brewing in Southeast Asia, we were now basically being warned that unless we were fully prepared to defeat communism, Laos was in its dangerous crosshairs.

In addition to these intelligence training and briefings, more physical training was part of our regimen. I had a foundation for some of these things from my prior training, but this program took it to a whole new level. The training was very similar to what Navy SEALS were put through. We ran in the water, swam, dove from great from heights, and swam to great depths. Fortunately for me, I liked the water, and I was a strong swimmer. Despite my strength, there was one time I almost did not make it during a long-distance swim. We would jump from a high place into deep water and then swim out far and simulate an attack on the enemy. We were tested on how long we could hold our breath under water. We trained in swimming pool first. We were taught to hold our breath and then release a bit of breath out a little at a time. I got to the point where I could hold my breath for a couple of minutes. We were then given a wetsuit and an oxygen tank and learned how to scuba dive. We really swam a lot! We were ordered to lie on the beach with whitewash running over us to see how long we could stay in the water. During the last six months of training, we jumped from planes into the water without gear. The purpose of the drill was to learn how to jump in the water properly. Over time, we piled on more and more gear before we jumped into the water. The purpose of that exercise was to make sure we would not drown with our gear on. Like something out of a James Bond movie, we were also instructed on how to use a one-man underwater motorized device. That device was like a seven-foot-long underwater jet ski that the enemy could not notice from above water.

We were instructed in advanced techniques on how to execute demolitions, the detonation of mines, how to use M67 grenade launchers to hit enemy territory, how to use combat knives with improved techniques, the use of body armor protection, night vision goggles, and bolt cutters. We were required to learn how to use a sniper rifle, along with machine guns and anti-tank weapons that could easily blow-up tanks. We were taught how to perform advanced emergency medicine treatment for battle wounds.

About two months before the year and a half of training was coming to an end, our training class was reminded of what we were told on day one: that the communists' goal was to end the monarchy rule in Laos. With that reminder, the CIA now told us that it was going to pull out from Laos and cut funding due to the problems back in the U.S. The officials did not get into the details. I was shocked. I did not think that U.S. support would be cut off completely. The CIA then told us, "When we cut out our support, you will use these techniques we have taught you to defend your country from the communists." I was then made an offer by the CIA. I was told, "Your country is going to change soon so we will bring you to the United States if you want." Despite the facts that were laid out before me, I loved my country. I had served my country with everything I had, and I just could not envision leaving. Despite the facts that were laid out before me, I still did not think the worst-case scenario would happen. I trusted my king and my prime minister. I wanted to believe that things would be OK.

While I was training during those last two months, I was hopeful that what the CIA was telling me about the political situation would not come to pass. Prior to the last two months, we were told this training was for us to prepare to fight the communists if it came to that. That time had come. We were being told that we had to fight, and we would be on our own. The CIA was telling us in no uncertain terms that it was up to us now to teach others to self-defend against the inevitability of a communist take-over. The top leaders said that the U.S. had internal political problems and that they would not be able to support us anymore. They told us the Royal Lao government and the communists had to work it out. I had a nagging feeling that the CIA knew this day was coming long before they revealed it to us.

While I was ready to fight until the very last bullet, I could not help but feel like our country was abandoned by the U.S. The promises that were made to us by the CIA made us believe they were behind us 100%. Now we had to face the reality that when the U.S. pulled its troops out of Southeast Asia, we would no longer be supported with ammunition, food, and equipment. We had sacrificed life as we knew it to battle the communists. Now we would soon have to fight them alone.

During my year and a half of training, I called my father twice. Since the cease fire agreement, he had not been fighting. While my father was high up in the military and even though he was not involved in the post-war negotiations, he could see that the politics were about to change in Laos. On my second call to my father, he said, "Our country is about to change. If the United States is pulling out their support, I do not know what way it is going to turn." My father's opinion at that time was that the U.S. pulling out was not a good thing for Laos. Like me, my father also got an offer from the U.S. Embassy to go to America. They had warned him things could get ugly in Laos. But, like me, my father refused. He would fight til the last because he loved his country. He also wanted to believe that our military was strong, that our King and Prime Minister were still in charge, and he did not believe the communists were going to be harmful to them. I mentioned to my father what I had learned about communism, how they will never recognize the monarchy, and they will wipe the royals out. "It will not be the way we think it will be," I told my father. My father said he did not know how it will be, but he would bring up the threat communism poses to the higher military command. If only everybody had listened.

Captain Ratanakone's uncle General Suradet Ratanakone (R) and his father General Khamphan Ratanakone (L).

Captain Ratanakone's uncle General Suradet Ratanakone sitting on the tank and his father General Khamphan Ratanakone standing on the tank.

Captain Ratanakone's father; General Khampan Ratanakone in front of a hut in the battlefield area in Xiang Khouang.

Captain Ratanakone's grandfather's funeral. Nai Ratanakone's remains are interred at the Louang Prabang Airport.

The young Captain Ratanakone saluting.

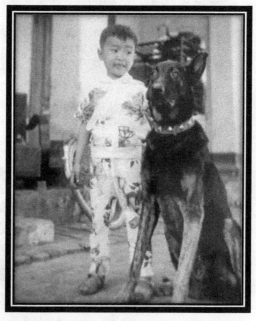

The young Captain Ratanakone and his dog named Big.

The young Captain Ratanakone holding a gun.

Captain Ratanakone stands ready to jump into battle.

143

Captain Ratanakone in uniform.

The types of Buddhas worn by Captain Ratanakone.

144

CHAPTER TWELVE

I finished my CIA training in the Philippines in September 1974 and returned home. When I came back, the political situation in Laos was as unstable as ever. I spoke to the House of Congress, and close to 400 people, including the King and the Prime Minister, were in attendance. Based on what I learned while working on behalf of the CIA, I wanted to inform them what the communist system was like and what harsh realities our country would face. I told them we should fight til the last. A subsequent meeting with about 600 people was held. Again, the argument was made to continue to fight the communists even after the U.S. pulled out. Everyone listened at both meetings, but the existing political realities may have interfered with what was best for the people of Laos. Our Prime Minister was Chao Souvanna Phouma, the head of the Neutralist Party. Souvanna Phouma had a younger half-brother, named Souphanouvong. Souvanna Phouma and Souphanouvong had the same father but different mothers. Souvanna Phouma wanted to avoid any conflict with the communists going back to1962. Souphanouvong attended school in Paris to study engineering. He then went to

Vietnam and became associated with Ho Chi Minh. Ho Chi Minh promised Souphanouvong that he would make him a leader of Laos and that the NVA would return to Vietnam.

Souphanouvong was then called a "red prince." He became a leader of the NVA and lived in the mountains in a cave at the border of Laos. Souphanouvong wanted to be a leader of Laos, wanted to stage a coup, and change the government. Souphanouvong was jailed and people who were on his side helped him escape. As an act of conciliation, the King gave two provinces, Houphan district and Pongsaly district, to Souphanouvong but he wanted more. A cease fire negotiation between the half-brothers was required so they would not kill each other. Souphanouvong's promise to Laos that the NVA would help them initially and then go back to Vietnam did not sit well with our generals. However, in the back of the generals' heads, they were satisfied if there would be no more fighting. Other generals never believed the NVA would just pack up and leave Laos. Nonetheless, the Lao government allowed some NVA to come into the city and let them join the government so they could work together. A small group believed the NVA would take over our country, but the majority wanted to believe that

Souvanna Phouma and Souphanouvong, two princes of Laos, would not allow the country to fall to the NVA. Our King also wanted to believe that the two brothers would work in the best interests of the Lao people. Souphanouvong promised that the communists would help him and that they had good intentions. The communists promised that the NVA would not shoot or harm any Lao royalists. They pointed to the 18 rules that were codified in the cease fire negotiations as evidence of their good intentions. Of course, they promised they would work for peace. The 18 rules, written in French and English, were agreed to by both sides, and 24 countries witnessed the signing of the cease fire and peace agreement in the Capitol house. It all sounded good.

Not long after these representations were made, Souphanouvang said to Souvanna Phouma, "We want your military men to go to a seminar. We also want the King, the royal family, the mayor all the government people, to go to a seminar to learn the new system of the communist government. Also, the military men need to give up their guns before they go to the seminar. After the training they will all get new guns that will be more powerful." When I learned of this, I believed they were falling for a lie, and that will never happen. The King and

Prime Minister did not believe the situation was suspicious or that the two brothers in power would not let our country fall.

The military men were told by Souphanouvang that this seminar would last for three months. They were told they were going to be sent to different parts of the country. Then, in June of 1975, the King was convinced to leave the capital. He was told that the people in the countryside had never seen a king before, so Souphanouvang requested that the King go visit them. The King went to the countryside, and he was put up in a small house. People lined up to visit the King, they bowed to him and pampered him. In return, the King gave money to the village, then he returned to the government house. He held a meeting and reported on his visit, and how much he enjoyed seeing the Laos people who were poor but friendly. Not long after that meeting, the King was told that the poor people in the villages wanted to see him again. This time, the King wanted to take his entire family. The Embassy in Laos warned the King they wanted to take him and his family out of the country for his safety because the situation in the country was precarious. But King would not listen to the warnings. He refused to leave Laos, insisted that nothing bad would happen and finally insisted, "I need to stay with my people." The King and his family then left to go to the countryside.

What I saw happening in Laos was very concerning to me. I was not alone in my belief that the communists were not going to do what they said. The communist military base was nearby the Royal Kingdom of Laos military base in the old capital city. They allowed the NVA to come into the Laos military bases. The two sides attempted to work together at first. I was involved in an event that showed the true colors of the communists. Some NVA military men came to the base where I was stationed at; I had been there since I returned home from my CIA training in the Philippines. As I was ordered, I accommodated the NVA and allowed them access to the base. However, when my men went to the NVA base nearby (the bases were approximately 20 to 30 meters apart) to inspect their set up, the NVA pointed the guns at my men and threatened to kill them. The NVA obviously had no intention of reciprocating or accommodating our military. When my men reported this incident to me, it seemed suspicious. The next time my men went to visit the NVA base, the NVA shot at them. One of my men was shot in the leg. They raced back to the base and reported the unprovoked attack to me. Without hesitation, I ordered them to shoot back at the NVA.

The skirmish that day resulted in nine of my men being injured and over 20 NVA being killed. The NVA leader complained to my superior officer and accused me of violating peace and neutrality. They lied and claimed that my men started the skirmish. The NVA demanded that I be severely punished for my actions. I told my superior officer to believe my story, not the NVA's version of events. The fact was that the NVA had attempted to kill our men first. I also made the case that this should put doubt in people's minds about the NVA's true intentions and their agenda for our country.

A big meeting was held about the conflicting stories about who started what. My men had reliable witnesses including the soldier who was shot in the leg. While I avoided jail, I was moved to a different base after the incident. Of course, the NVA was very upset at the Kingdom of Laos for not doing anything to significantly punish me. For the first time, I now thought about leaving my country. I spoke to my father again after this incident. My father insisted, "We have to fight til the last, and do our best first. We can't give up and be the first to leave for the United States." For the first time, I argued with my father about this issue. Usually, I am not argumentative, but I was arguing now because of the CIA perspective I had learned. I believed I had the proper insight into communist mindset. In the end, I respected his father's military and political experience so I resolved to hope that things would be better than I expected. I also had to accept that I could not contact the CIA at that time unless I crossed over to the U.S. Embassy in Thailand. I also had to respect my father's wishes that the whole family was in Laos and we owed it to them and our people to fight til the last if necessary.

In July of 1975, the U.S. military finally pulled out from Thailand, South Vietnam, and the border of Laos. Our country was officially on its own and vulnerable to whatever plans the NVA had for us. The NVA declared to us that Laos had lost to the NVA leaders. At this point a lot of the NVA military were in every department of the Laos government. We were now under their control.

My father was told he had to go the three-month seminar, or "training" as the NVA also called it. The NVA repeated that the reason for the training was to understand the 18 rules set forth in the peace agreement between the NVA and the Royal Lao Military, how the NVA and Laos would work together and co-exist in peace.

My father accepted this reason, told our family he would see us in three months and off he went in a cargo truck with other military men.

Two weeks later, on a Tuesday morning in late July of 1975, I dressed in my uniform and told my mother I was going to the military base. When I arrived, I was told that I had to go to the three-month training. Based on the training I had already received from the CIA, and the recent skirmish I had on the NVA military base, I was skeptical about the truth behind this training. However, higher ranked officers than me, including my own father, and the politicians were willingly going. I was not allowed to gather any belongings or tell my mother that I was leaving. Usually, I would return home for lunch, so I knew my mother would be worried. Meanwhile, back at home, my mother was indeed worried when I did not come home. Her instinct was that I was going to be taken away to a "training seminar" just as my father had two weeks earlier. She wanted to give me food before I left so she packed up sticky rice, beef jerky and chili and rushed to the military base to bring me the food for the journey.

I was rounded up with about 600 other officers. We were put in cargo trucks and driven to the airport. We had no idea where we were going. We were divided into groups and put on either C30 or C-31 planes. My group boarded a C-31 plane and soon learned we were headed to the city of Ponesavanh in the southern province of Xiengkhouang. We arrived at about 1:30 in the afternoon. All 600 of us were ordered by the NVA to start walking. We all were loaded down with our full military gear which weighed about 60 pounds. Our guns had been taken away from us. We did not stop walking until 5 a.m. the next morning. The NVA finally allowed us to rest for about two hours. Fortunately, I had the food my mother had given me, so I shared it with some of my fellow soldiers. We still had no idea as to where we were going.

After a couple of hours of rest, we were ordered to start walking again. Before we started, though, we were lined up in front of a large and deep crater created from bombing during the war. We were then ordered told to take off our medals (we were still in full uniform), every item of our gear (except our backpacks) and throw them into the crater. We were told to do this because none of those things were going to be of any use to us anymore. Any doubts any of us had about the communists' true intentions were now cleared up: all of us were prisoners.

CHAPTER THIRTEEN

We all started to walk again at 7 a.m. We trudged through the jungle for a day and a half straight. During the exhausting journey, I thought about my father and how he had most certainly suffered the same fate as we did. I wondered where he was now. I wondered if he, too, was thinking about the grave error in judgement that was made by the leadership of Laos. It was a grave mistake to believe the lies of the communists. We were all told we were going to a seminar to learn the new communist system. We were all tricked into thinking everything would be good and we would all get along.

No water or food was given to us during the march through the jungle. I continued to share what food I had left from what my mother had given me. When we saw water in nearby creeks or rivers, we would drink from them. At 9 p.m. the next evening, we reached the village of Someneua in the Houaphan district. The village was a Lao communist base with bamboo huts. There were big pots with boiling rice in them. After being fed some meager portions of rice, we were allowed to sleep. Any ideas of us being allowed to sleep in those huts were dashed immediately. We had to lay our backpacks on the ground and sleep on them. In this area there were leeches in the trees. When we were all woken up by the Lao communists, we saw we had been bloodied by the leeches feeding on us.

The Lao communists then walked around and gave us a piece of paper and a pencil. They ordered us to write down our first and last name, rank in the military and details about ourselves. They told us to tell the truth and tell them exactly what we did for Laos in the military. They emphasized that we should admit if we ever killed any NVA soldiers or communists. They promised that if we told the truth then we would be able to go home first.

With 600 of us prisoners having served in the Lao military during the past years of war, of course we had all killed NVA. I was never going to admit that to them. I had been trained to never tell the enemy the truth. In my "history," I wrote down a fake name. I chose "Nak Ounkham." I came up with that name because I was born in the dragon year, and Nak means dragon. I chose "Ounkham" because that was my mother's maiden name. I claimed that I never killed any NVA or communists, that I worked an office job and that I was never sent to the battlefield. Most of the other prisoners also lied, however, some did tell the truth. Those prisoners who told the truth believed the communists once again and hoped they would be the first to go home. After the Lao communists gathered our information and looked it over, they separated us into groups. Those who admitted to killing NVA were placed into one group and those who wrote down that they did not kill any NVA were put into another group.

Those of us who said we had never killed any NVA, which was around 500 men, were moved to a new holding area in Na Dan. As for the 100 or so men who told the truth, we never saw them again. It again confirmed that the plan of the communists all along was to punish those who fought against the NVA. We then walked about 25 minutes to go to a new area. The Lao communists ordered us to clean up this area. We had to clean the area only using large leaves. When we were done with this strenuous task, we were gathered for another meeting with the Lao communists. They said we could ask them questions if we had any. I quietly warned some fellow prisoners sitting next to me not to ask any questions at all. This was the Lao communists' twisted way to see if we would question their authority or go against them. Sure enough, the ones who asked questions were separated from the group and they were killed. There was a killing field nearby, where the Lao communists took prisoners out and executed them. There were no burials.

What happened next was that we were handed dull machetes. As I sharpened my machete by the river, I saw a stamp on it indicating it was made in Cuba. We were ordered to chop trees to make huts and make a camp. In August of 1975, we were then ordered to dig a deep hole. It had to be 20 feet by 20 feet, and 4 feet deep. A ramp was built to enter and exit the hole. We had to cut the trees then we stacked logs all around the hole, like a wall surrounding it. The deep hole was covered with logs. That is where we were held as prisoners. The Lao communists always guarded the hole. When it rained, water would rush down the ramp. Many times, water would fill the hole and come up to our necks. It was not unusual for someone to die from drowning. Every two weeks, we were permitted to leave the hole to get fresh air. Once, during this time away from the hole, two dead bodies were discovered. One time, for no reason, the Lao communist guards screamed at me, "The dog CIA, you are a dog, you are working for CIA, this is what you get!" They hit me in the neck with the butt of the gun. I passed out from the blow, too weak from not enough food.

At first, we prisoners would talk softly among ourselves. From word of mouth from the other prisoners, I learned the Lao communists had set up five different camps. They would separate different groups into different camps. The royal family was imprisoned in one camp, political people were imprisoned in another camp and military people, based on their rank, were imprisoned in the other camps. I heard about other people being killed in the camps from other prisoners who were brought into our camp. I would hear about torturing and killing of prisoners, like those who were dragged around by a jeep until they died. I thought about my father, and whether he was still alive.

Soon, talking among us was forbidden. When the Lao communists heard the whispering, they dragged people out of the hole, accused them of planning to escape and then killed them. After that, there would be no talking. We would just stare at each other in dreaded silence. My CIA training helped get me through this monotony. I recalled my training class where I learned to meditate and concentrate on positive things. I willed myself to live and not die like a rat. The concentration camp was up in the mountains. We were given two meals a day and calling them "meals" was an exaggeration because it was just small bowl of horrible tasting rice soup. Sometimes we were allowed to leave, guarded of course, to look for food. When I climbed up a tree, I could see a village down below, with smoke rising from fires cooking food. That sight would give me hope that one day, somehow, I could get back to my home. I dreamed of seeing my family again. I imagined coming home and eating coconuts and sticky rice again. I used these thoughts to focus on getting out of this concentration camp someday and that I would do anything to survive.

After four months, the NVA allowed us to come out every two weeks and get fresh air and sun for 15 minutes at a time. Still, we were very weak from lack of nutrition. When we were able to leave the hole, we were so weak that we had to crawl out. In the confined space of the hole was where we ate, slept, and used as a bathroom. We were given water with our meals and it was the only water we received. If we wanted to clean ourselves, we had to choose between using the water for drinking or cleaning. During the year that we were confined to that hole, seven of the 25 prisoners died. I do not know how many of the other 475 prisoners died. I do know that there were beatings every day. Offending prisoners were tied to a pole. Not only were they beaten and made to sleep while tied up, but they were also spit on and yelled at every day. They were accused of working for the CIA. They were told, "You will be here until you die. You were stupid to work for the CIA."

The Lao communists constantly asked the prisoners if they knew anybody in the group who worked for the CIA or who killed NVA soldiers. The Lao communists promised us that if anybody identified someone who worked for the CIA, they would be set free and could go home. I assumed that the Lao communists always knew I was in the CIA. I would have thought that everybody had learned by now not to tell a communist the truth about anything. Unfortunately, a military school classmate who served with me during the battle at Attapeu, cracked under the pressure and fell for that lie. He told the Lao communists about me, that I was a captain in the army and that I had killed NVA soldiers. I was dragged out of the deep hole and a Lao communist guard yelled at me, "I know who you are and who you work for! You killed our men in that battle!" I stuck to the story I wrote in my history. I said I was a military man, but I never killed anybody because I only worked on the military base. I went even further with my story and said I did paperwork, worked in the office, paid bills, and made sure military officers got their salary. The Lao communist guard accused me three times. During the third time, the guard brought my friend with him so he could positively identify me. My friend said to me, "You know, man, why don't you just go ahead and tell the truth so we can both go home? You and me we used to be in the battle together, killing them together. Let's tell the truth." Before this day, I had spoken with this person about what to do if this scenario played out. However, the Lao communists seemed to have broken this person mentally. He kept asking me before this day, "Why don't we tell them the truth so we can go home?" I repeatedly told him, "They lied to you to get you to this torture camp. You still believe them? You think they will let you go? If we tell them the truth, we will be killed." On this day, when my friend again asked me to tell the truth in front of our captors, I acted upset as I said, "I don't know you. I never knew you. We both might have been in the military, but I never went out and killed anybody." I was so convincing in my denial that the Lao communists believed me. The guard turned to my friend and said, "You lied to us." The NVA guard shot my friend, and I watched his brains get blown out. This was a disturbing sight, to be sure. I had to lie, though. This was life or death, so I did not break the rule of the Buddha monk. Even if there was no Buddha monk rule to obey, I knew that if I told the truth, I would have been shot in the head. I knew one of us would be killed, but I also knew the one who always got killed was the one who believed the communists.

I was still interrogated a couple of times after that. The guards took me out and asked the same questions. I always repeated that I never knew my friend who was killed, and that I never was in a battle. A guard would pull out a gun, slam it against my head and say, "If you lie, I'm going to kill you right now like I killed your friend!" I would say back to him, "Go ahead, I'm telling the truth so kill me if you want to." I had trained myself to think, "If I'm going to die, I'll die." I knew that if I changed my answer now, I would be killed anyway. The Lao communists never found anyone else who could identify me, like my dead friend did. I always told many of my fellow prisoners never to tell the communists the truth. Unfortunately, many of them refused to listen to me.

There were other forms of psychological warfare that were used on us daily. Guards would come in every day and curse at us. "You are dumb, you are stupid, you have no brains, we will find out you are CIA and then kill you and your family." They said whatever they could to break us mentally. It was an unlikely option, but escape was always on my mind. I tried to escape a couple of times when I thought I had a chance. For example, there was the time that the Lao communists took us out to blow up a mountain to make a road. They forced us to do everything by hand when machines were really needed for such a massive job. All we had to use was a hammer and chisel to break up the rocks. After breaking up the rock we placed the explosive in it. Accidents were always happening. When the explosives were detonated, flying rocks and rubble would kill people. There were prisoners working above me and below me on the mountain. During the work, someone dropped a hammer, it hit someone on the head and killed them. The Lao communists would force us to work at three in the morning and we could not see what we were doing in the darkness. One night, I waited for an explosion to go off. I made myself tumble down the mountain. My plan was to then attempt to escape. When I reached the bottom, there was a Lao communist guard right there. I acted like my fall down the mountain was an accident caused by the explosion. It was another close call that I got away with. While I felt like I was protected by my Buddha Master, and I knew how to lie convincingly to my captors, I also wondered how long my luck would last.

CHAPTER FOURTEEN

In August of 1976, my days of being confined to the deep hole were over. 18 of the original 25 prisoners in my hole had survived so far. One day, the Lao communists came down to the hole and asked me questions. They were looking for someone who could be a handy person, who could drive different kinds of vehicles, who could speak English and who could be mechanical. I said I could do it all, even though they did not say what they needed me for exactly. I then learned I was going to be relocated. Some of us were going to be assigned to build roads and some of us were going to be making rice fields. Of course, all the work was going to be done by hand with inadequate tools.

Along with many other prisoners, we left Someneua. I came out of the deep hole for the last time with chains on my ankles. I was always in shackles at this point. To this day, I still have scars on both sides of my ankles. The wounds were a result of the shackles rubbing against my skin. Not only would my skin get ripped off, but bugs and worms would get into the fresh wounds and infect them. I suffered from multiple infections yet, of course, the communists never treated them. I healed the wounds myself. I placed dirt on my wet skin to keep the bugs away. I would also use leaves to rub the wounds to dry them out. I knew that liquid from certain soft leaves were medicinal. If the type of liquid was helpful, it would feel cool on the wound. If the feeling from the liquid was hot, I would know not to use that type of leaf. An excellent healing plant was "farung," which was a little white flower on top of big, tall grass. I learned this healing trick from my military training.

One night after waking all day in shackles we stopped at a spot to sleep. It was a cold night. The Lao communists signaled to us by banging something metal to pick up firewood to start a bonfire. As we gathered firewood, the guards ordered us where to put the wood. The time had come to light up the firewood and then go to sleep. I could not get a spot to sleep near the big bonfire because so many prisoners were crowded around the same area. I decided to build my own bonfire which was about 150 yards away. A few of us were lying around the smaller bonfire that we had built when a huge explosion shook the ground and blew us up into the air. I felt the compression in my chest, then blacked out. I was not sure how long I was unconscious for, but when I came to, there was smoke everywhere. I could make out the bloody body parts scattered all over the place. Others did not die right away and bled to death from their lost limbs. It turns out this area had a lot of leftover bombs that the U.S. military dropped from B-52 planes during the war. Many of the bombs were still active even though they had not detonated. The Lao communists knew this, just as they knew the heat from the bonfire would detonate the bomb. Those of us who survived felt lucky to be alive. Another odd thing happened to me, though. For the next three days, even though there was little food to be had anyway, I did not feel hungry at all.

The group I was in was assigned to turn jungle land into a rice field. The work was to be done while our feet were shackled so we could not escape. Our first task was to build huts where we would live during the job. Each hut was made so it could fit 50 to 60 of us. Building these huts took about a month. Each hut was just a big room with a walkway in the middle and rows of bunks raised a foot off the ground on each side. Even though we were building living quarters a step up from the deep pit, our existence was still very poor and still that of prisoners. Our bathroom was a big hole about six feet deep with a log on top to sit on. There was a river about 25 minutes away where we would sometimes be allowed to clean ourselves. We had to find our own food in the jungle most of the time. Each hut had its own Lao communist guard who would decide which of us would do what task. Usually, two of us would go out to look for food and then three or four of us would cook whatever was brought back. We had to do that because, before we made the rice fields, the tiny bowls of rice that the communists gave us was old, smelled horribly and was always infested with little bugs. When we were served this terrible meal, the rice grains floated alongside the bugs and expired milk powder. Many prisoners died from diarrhea because they ate this inedible food. One of my fellow prisoners, Captain Somkeo, was older than me. Due to poor health and malnutrition, he broke down and cried out, "I am the only person who supported my family! Without me, how will they survive?!" I knew Captain Somkeo had left his parents, wife and two children after he was tricked into going to the concentration camp. Even though I was younger than him and was not married, I was still in the same boat as him. All I knew to tell him was that we could not show weakness to our captors. I urged him to keep his thoughts to himself and hopefully we would escape this situation and see our families again someday.

Armed with a dull machete, my fellow prisoners and I would go into the jungle in search of food. Mushrooms, if they were not poisonous, were a staple. I would look for trees and bushes that bugs would be likely to eat. If the tree was not touched by bugs, then one had to assume it could be poisonous. Even if fruit was growing all over tree, if no bugs or animals ate the fruit, then I stayed away from it. I looked for trees where fruit was on the ground half eaten by animals. Banana and bamboo trees were good sources of food because one could eat the inside of the trunks or the leaves. We would also cut the tree trunks to bring back to the camp and make soup. The Lao communists had salt in big rock form from China that we would smash up and add to the soup.

I also looked for edible roots, but that took real work. The search for these roots sometimes required me to dig deep in the ground. The reason I had to do that was because the top part was tough to eat and could cause a bad allergic reaction. One time, I was so hungry and weak, I went out and dug for the younger part of the root. I had to dig very deep for the younger root, about three or four feet. Unfortunately, I did not bother to make the hole very wide. I put my head down in the hole to search for the root and my head got stuck in the hole. With just my feet being visible, I yelled for help, but no one could hear me. Finally, the other prisoners that were out looking for food finally found me and pulled me out of the hole.

It was hard to avoid getting sick from the terrible food situation. Some prisoners even died from the food. The problem was that no one wanted to admit they were sick. If someone got sick or had a fever and the communists found out about it, they would accuse that person of being lazy. The communists would then inject the sick people a shot of some kind of medicine, but they would usually only live for about two to three weeks after that.

After our shacks were built, we were then ordered to start work on turning the jungle land into a rice field. A typical day started at three in the morning. We were given a dull machete then would walk for about an hour until we got the area we had to work. The traditional way of preparing a rice field was to plow the ground during the monsoon season. Cows were usually used to pull a plow to make ground soft. In our primitive situation, we prisoners were the cows. Four or five of us would construct our own plow using sticks and rope. We would plow the soil then we had to use a stick to dig into the ground to bury the rice. We worked every day until 10 o'clock at night.

Even though we planted the rice, we never got to eat it. We were never sure where the communists took the rice. I figured it was used to supply their military. It made me wonder that if the rice was for their people, they should have given us better equipment to use to plant it. The communists also took time to remind us why we were prisoners in the first place. While we toiled in the field, guards would yell at us, "Look at you now! You are the workers from the CIA so you guys will die, and no one will help you! This is what you get for serving the United States!"

While I was able to search for food and was out in the field, I thought there was no safe chance to try to escape at that time. The areas always had guards on the perimeter to prevent an escape. That is not to say that many prisoners thought they could escape and made attempts. Those foolish enough to try under these conditions always got caught. Some of the 35 offenders were not killed right away. They would be tied to a flagpole for a week with no food and maybe some water was given to them. Some would be put back into the deep hole. The rumor was that those who were killed were executed in the rice field.

During the monsoon season in June or July of 1977, I was working in the rice fields with other prisoners, digging and plowing the ground. The water came up to my knees while I worked. Normally, this work would be done with the help a cow and or horses. I only had one dull shovel to plow and dig with. My whole body was shaking with every motion because it took so much effort to dig up the ground. There was a guard standing by to give us signals when to dig. That guard would then blow the whistle signaling for us to plow the ground. I was very weak and exhausted. Sometime around noon, I passed out, face down in the water. I ingested a lot of dirty water. I have no idea how long I was unconscious for. When the guards dragged me to higher ground, they were pumping my chest until I threw up the dirty water. I remember one of my prisoner friends kept saying to me, "You coming back? You coming back?" He was repeating this question because I was near death. I also remember thinking when the guards would serve us our meager lunch because I was so hungry. I was soon semi-conscious enough to talk. The guards allowed me to rest a bit. I put one hand over my head and thought I was going to die that day. I thought I was feeling death and I would never get to see my family again. I had even less strength than I did while I was working in the flooded field. The lunch I had been wishing for finally arrived. The guards put the horrible rice soup with China salt next to me. I tried to eat it but was unable to because I had thrown up so much dirty water. At that moment, for the first time, I had no hope.

I unexpectedly got a reprieve from the harsh work in the rice fields. Colonel Dao Phet, who was a Lao tribal man-turned-communist, was going for training in Vientiane for the next six months. He was about 72 years old, but he had taken a bride who was only 26 years old. He needed someone to watch over and assist his wife. Colonel Phet requested that I be the one to take care of his wife for him. Why did he pick me? I believe it was because I established good relations with his family and I had offered to help him in the past. I helped with house repairs, raising his chickens and pigs, and doing farm work. For example, the Colonel's house had one side that was tilted. I offered to help him fix it. Another time, I helped him plant a garden. Colonel Phet saw that I was an honest man. He would ask me about finding medicine for him. I would always be able to help him out and I earned his trust.

Colonel Phet lived in a nice bamboo house. It was the type of house that only communist leaders enjoyed. It was a raised-up house with an enclosed bedroom and the rest of the house was an open patio area. There was a room for the Colonel's wife to sleep and I would sleep outside on the patio on a mattress. Not only was this work assignment unexpected, but so were the gestures the Colonel's wife made towards me. She was in her 20's, very pretty and was from the tribal town of Thaidam. She tried to have me sleep in her room while her husband was gone. She told me that she wanted to be massaged and to have a "partner." The Colonel's wife then grabbed my hand and put it on her breasts. I said that she could not do that, and I could not be with her like that. She ignored what I said. Instead, she said she would never tell her husband, that she would protect me and make sure no harm would come to me. Without a second thought, I told her I would not do what she asked. I left right away even though it was the middle of the night and walked an hour and a half back to the camp. I was stopped by the communist guards, and they asked me where I was coming from. I told them I was coming back from watching over Colonel Phet's house. The guards were aware of my assignment, and they walked me back to the concentration camp without incident. Upon returning to the camp, I asked to speak to another Colonel and I told him exactly what had happened at Colonel Phet's house.

Two days later, the Lao communists selected another prisoner to go to Colonel Phet's house. That prisoner happened to be a friend of mine named Dauangchan. He reminded me of my friend Bounchanh; a tall, good-looking man who had always had many girlfriends before he became a prisoner of war. I warned Dauangchan not to go to Colonel Phet's. I knew that he would get in trouble and probably get killed because Colonel Phet's pretty wife would try to seduce him. Dauangchan assured me he would watch himself and not get into any trouble. I told Dauangchan that if he did not heed my warning, he would certainly be killed. Dauangchan again told me not to worry, he would not do anything to bring himself any harm. My final warning to him was, "Dauangchan, I know you. Once you see her, you will forget that you promised anything." A few months after Dauangchan moved into Colonel Phet's house, the colonel's wife became pregnant with Dauangchan's baby. When Colonel Phet found out about this, he put Dauangchan in the deep hole for a week. When

Dauangchan was let out of the hole, the Lao communists beat him to death.

Following Dauangchan's death, Colonel Phet summoned me to meet with him. Even though I had done nothing wrong, I was nervous about this meeting. Colonel Phet wanted to know why I had left his house. I knew that I always had to lie to the communists, but in this case I knew I had to tell the truth. I explained to Colonel Phet exactly what happened so he would know for sure that it was not me who got his wife pregnant. After I told him everything, Colonel Phet admitted that despite what had happened, he still loved his wife. He then told me I was a good and honest man. He promised that he would do his best to help me out whenever I needed it. Then he said he needed to have a heart-to-heart talk with me. He needed my help. I had no idea how I could possibly help him, but I said I would do my best. Colonel Phet asked me if he could help him with his wife, her needs and his "ability." I understood what he needed and assured him that I knew what could help him.

While I was working in the jungle near the Ho Chi Minh trail near a deep mountain area, I noticed there was a big tree with an unusual plant growing high up there. I also noticed when the Chinese communist soldiers cut the tree down, they rushed to find and collect these plants on the tree. I figured it must be something very valuable to the Chinese people. By way of background, after the war the Chinese constantly came to Laos to get certain natural resources. China was near North Vietnam, and it did not have the quality of resources, like trees, that Laos had. Trucks came in from North Vietnam and China, soldiers would blow up the mountain and took away the dirt day and night. I saw Chinese soldiers working near a mountain and it smelled like gas or raw eggs. It looked like they were probably mining for Sulphur. They blew up the mountain, dug with heavy duty equipment and put soil in the truck. They would also cut big trees from the jungle and took them away in trucks back to China. I noticed many Chinese communist soldiers picking a particular herbal plant out from the ground around certain trees. I asked them in English what the plant was for. "For food?" I asked. "Do you eat it?" They laughed, answered in Chinese but used hand gestures that made me understand right away it was meant to help them with their "ability." In other words, it was would be considered today as an herbal "Viagra" drug. They explained that they soaked the plant in rice whiskey or boiled it in water. When the color of the liquid turned black, they would drink it.

To help Colonel Phet, I was permitted to go into the jungle and find this plant. I returned to Colonel Phet's house and prepared the drink for him. I took only a tiny sip first, only to make sure it was safe for him to drink and not poisonous. It had a bitter and sweet taste. Then I gave it to Colonel Phet to drink. By the third day of drinking this liquid, he informed me that he was so happy and felt he was re-born again. Colonel Phet thanked me over and over for helping him with his wife. He reminded me that he would always be there to help me. Despite what happened while he was away, Colonel Phet ended up taking care of the baby. Despite my training to always lie to the communists, the truth worked for me this time, kept me alive and would help me in the future.

CHAPTER FIFTEEN

In 1977, at the Na Ghai concentration camp where I was a prisoner, 178 Lao Kingdom military officers were brought in from all over the country. These were men who had initially refused to surrender their weapons and attend the "training seminar." When they arrived, the Lao communists announced to them that, "You lost." Once the 178 military men realizcd they had been tricked into being at the camp, they decided to walk out. The Lao communists said, "If you walk out, we will kill you all." I knew what these military men were thinking. They figured they either die today or endure being tortured by the communists and dying another day; it was just a matter of time of when they were going to be killed by the enemy. In an act of unity, all 178 military officers marched out of the camp. True to their word, the Lao communists killed them all. The Lao communists then told all of us, "That is the future of stupid people who were helped the CIA and the United States." They pointed to the 178 dead military men and said, "You can bury them or leave bodies there for the animals to eat. We don't care." I joined other prisoners to help bury my dead brothers-in-arms as best as we could. These sons of Laos were all educated, went to military schools, and loved their country with all their heart and blood. I helped bury them with tears in my heart.

In May of 1977, the Lao communist ordered me and others to go to a mountainous village called Sanakhan to look for food. The reason we were sent there was because the villagers had escaped from Laos to Thailand. They had fled because of the fighting and the fear of living under the oppressive rule of the Lao communists. As a result of them fleeing, their village was now abandoned. When the Lao communists heard that the village was empty, they wanted to search the village for food and supplies. About 200 men from our concentration camp were ordered to travel to the abandoned village. Lao communist guards were placed in front of us, behind us and spread out in the middle of us. As we walked to Sanakhan, we passed the city of Mueangviengxai in the district of Houphan. This was where the concentration camp was that held prisoners who were part of the Royal Family as well as high-ranking military officers who were generals. The Royal Family was imprisoned on one side of the camp and the high-ranking officers were imprisoned on the other side of the camp. As we were walking, I spotted a man and a woman who were pulling weeds as part of a rice planting. Both were skinny and pale. Some Lao communist guards were watching over them from a nearby hut house. I was about 50 to 75 feet away from this couple. The woman then turned to look at me. I immediately recognized her as Queen Khamphoui of Laos. I then recognized the man as her husband, King Sisavang. When I saw it was our King and Queen, I signaled my men of this fact. We all sat on our knees and put our hands together to pay our respects. The Queen looked at us and realized we must be from Laos. She turned to her husband. The King dropped his hoe. He said loud enough for us to hear, "Don't do that! You will be killed." The Queen could be heard saying, "My poor men." They both looked so sad. The guards who were with us demanded to know what we were doing. They said, "What are you stupid people doing? Keep walking." I said, "They are our king and queen." A guard screamed at me, "There is no king or queen anymore! Pretty soon I will kill you, too!" That was a sure give away to me that the King and Queen would not survive.

During the summer of 1977, two other prisoners and I were looking for food out in the forest to supply the entire concentration camp. We were looking for vegetables, banana trunk, and leaves to make soup or to serve as food for everyone in the camp There was a kitchen in a bamboo hut where prisoners ate. At that time, our communist captors allowed families to visit the prisoners. When I got back to the camp, there were dead people everywhere. The Lao communists poisoned the food of the families and prisoners. There were about 50 people who were killed. Many of them were lying dead in the kitchen. None of the Lao communists died because they did not eat the food. The Lao communists then blamed the wife of a prisoner who came in to visit for poisoning everyone. I knew they were lying. I had to help bury the dead. I remember burying a child who was only six or seven years old. My thoughts of escape intensified.

After spending two years as a prisoner in the concentration camp, I had not yet had what I thought was a good chance to make an escape. In August of 1977, I finally had that chance. At that time, I was one of a group of 13 men out looking for food. We all had machetes with us. Instead of returning to the camp, we took a chance, and successfully evaded the guards. We switched between running and walking for two days and two nights. We were getting close to reaching a village when we were caught by the Lao communists. They lined us all up, tied our hands around our neck, shackled all 13 of us together and marched us back to the camp. When we returned to camp, it went from bad to worse quickly. All of us were tied up to a flagpole for 26 days, although we were still fed twice a day. We were then placed back into the deep hole again. One time they put me, and another prisoner named Captain Khambang, into a giant leech pool for about 45 minutes. Since we were weak and numb from being tied up to the flagpole, we were not able to move much in the water. Meanwhile, the leeches in the water covered our bodies, sucked our blood until they were too heavy and finally dropped off from our body. By the time that the Lao communist guards lifted us out, the water was bloody, and we were covered in blood from head to toe.

We were confined to the deep hole for about eight months. Every two weeks we could crawl out to get some sun and fresh air. Six of my fellow prisoners died during this time. After serving our time in the hole, the surviving seven of us were brought out. We were handed shovels and were told to dig a hole for ourselves We were told to decide how deep we wanted it because we were digging our own grave. I was the second prisoner in the row while we were digging our graves. The third prisoner right next to me whispered to me, "If you are alive, please don't forget to tell my parents that I died so they can do good for me." I said to him, "Why are you asking me this? It looks like we are all going to die." The third prisoner said he did not think they would kill me. I thought it was strange that he would think that.

After we dug our graves, we were all blindfolded. I recall just feeling numb. I heard the "bam" of a gun. I could hear the first prisoner to one side of me drop to the ground. I heard the Lao communist guard's footsteps walk near me. I prayed that if this was my time to die, I wanted to return to a life where there was no pain and just peace. It then felt like something was running through my body that made me shake. I believed it was the presence of my Master, the Buddha monk who had put the tattoos on me. I heard another gunshot. The third prisoner on the other side of me dropped dead. Then I counted off four more shots. I heard some of my fellow prisoners calling out for their families after being shot or right before they were shot. It was torture to think about was happening. When the gunshots stopped, the blindfold was ripped off me. I saw the other six prisoners were dead. I touched my own body to make sure I was still alive. Then I saw Colonel Phet standing there. He gave me a look as I was led away by the guards.

I later learned that it was only because of Colonel Phet that my life was spared. He told the other communists that I was not a hardheaded man. He told them that I was not the ringleader of the escape, that I could not possibly be a leader and I probably just followed all the rest of them out of the concentration camp. Colonel Phet finally said that I was a good but simple man who would not hurt anyone.

Colonel Phet met with me after my near-death experience after the escape attempt. Believe it or not, my first reaction was that I got angry at him. If he wanted to save me, why not get me released from the concentration camp? The whole experience was slowly killing me anyway. Colonel Phet was very understanding, and he calmed me down. He promised he would ask for permission for me to leave the camp and go to the capital, even though he was certain those requests would be denied. I calmed down, kneeled before Colonel Phet, bowed before him, and thanked him for saving my life. Colonel Phet then lowered his voice and told me to save my dry rice. "Save your supply," he said, "I believe you will need it in the future. You never know what a good day will be." Colonel Phet was in essence saying that he would always try his best to protect me but at some point, I would have to help myself and try to escape again. I listened to his advice and I started to dry my rice.

Colonel's Phet's kind regard for me in front of his fellow communist officers may have helped me in another way. Colonel Khamdong, who was from the Kha tribe, took a liking to me as well. He asked me to help work in his rice field, raise his pigs and chickens, and assist him with other things around his house. He also had a daughter who was about 16 years old.

Colonel Khamdong told his daughter that if she had a hard-working man like me, she would always be taken care of. Colonel Khamdong wanted me to be his daughter's future husband. However, I was not interested in this arrangement. If I dared go through with such a thing, I would have to become a communist and that was never going to happen. I wanted to stay out of the concentration camp and keep Colonel Khamdong happy, so I kept working hard for him. That still did not stop him from trying to marry me off to his daughter. He set up one small room in his house for me and his daughter to sleep in. His daughter would go to work with me in the field every day and then we would sleep in the same room at night. This went on for three months. I did not make any overtures towards his daughter. Colonel Khamdong asked his daughter every day if I tried to be intimate with her. She told her father I had not tried anything, and she thought that maybe I did not like girls. Colonel Khamdong went so far as to offer me the same kind of "Viagra herb" that I got for Colonel Phet! I was not going to be tricked and I threw it away. I knew what Colonel Khamdong was trying to do.

Colonel Khamdong tried a different and more direct approach. He told me he would support me if I was with his daughter. He offered to send me to military school in Russia and Vietnam so I could work for the communists. He was thinking that they would welcome someone like me because I was honest, hardworking, and smart. However, from my CIA training, I knew that if I went down such a path, the communists would want to use me to spy on anti-communists in Laos. While I would never consider accepting Colonel Khamdong's offer, I tried a different approach as well. I asked if I could go back home to visit my family before I made any decisions. Colonel Khamdong tried to get permission to send me to back to Vientiane, but the Lao communists would not allow it.

While I was living with Colonel Khamdong, I noticed many of the prisoners' wives and children were now allowed to visit the camp. Secured fences 20 yards apart separated the prisoners and visitors. There were guards on both sides of the fences. Word had spread about the existence of the concentration camps so that was why visitors were allowed. Of course, the communists decided who could visit and who could not. Families would bribe the guards with gold, money, or jewels to be allowed to visit their husband and/or father. I would later learn that my cousin's father paid two kilograms of gold to have his son released from the camp. I was not in any position to have my family visit, from a bribe or otherwise, because I had used a fake name when I gave the communists my history back in 1975. My family would have no idea where I was now. For all I knew, they believed that I was dead.

During the supervised visits, prisoners and their wives could talk briefly. The wife would bring things from home for her husband. The prisoner's family could stay in a hut house located on the family side of the fence. The true intention behind this arrangement was horrible. The Lao communist leader of the camp, if he liked a prisoner's wife, would put her in a separate hut so he could sleep with her. There was a time when I was talking to other prisoners. One prisoner said, "I don't know when I can go back home. I saw my wife briefly. We didn't even talk much." Then two guards that worked under the Lao communist leader came by and said, "You are a stupid idiot, CIA man. Our leader slept with your wife!" The prisoner collapsed in shock and grief, knocked his head, and passed out. When the prisoner came to, he asked me what happened to him. I had to remind him that he was told that the Lao communist leader slept with his wife. This prisoner had been a captain during the war, and he fought honorably to protect his country, but there was absolutely nothing he could do to protect his wife. This prisoner broke down in tears. I could feel his pain and tried to calm him down. It was impossible for this man to hold his tears back. It was clearer than ever what the communists' intentions were: to kill us and to hurt us, not only physically and but also to cut our hearts out emotionally and spiritually. I kept telling this man, "It's not your fault. There's nothing we can do. Don't hurt yourself. Think positively that one day you will see your wife again."

After spending time with this poor man, I went back out into the field to work. I was not there long when I broke down and cried my heart out. When the communists slept with prisoners' wives, they made sure the prisoner knew. Some prisoners could not handle this torture. They would suffer a mental breakdown, they would talk to themselves or cut their own throat or hang themselves. Many prisoners died physically and mentally. I wanted to believe that maybe the communists were playing mind games with the prisoners, and maybe they had not really slept with the prisoners' wives. I was grateful I had not gotten married or that my girlfriend had no idea where I was. Years later, for those of us who survived the camps, some former prisoners spoke to their wife or girlfriend, and they learned it was true. The women could not discuss it at the time because they were warned if they did, their men would be killed.

CHAPTER SIXTEEN

My CIA training about the psychology of the communist way of thinking was exactly as they had taught us. Understanding the enemy's point of view, as inhumane as it was, helped me survive. While I would never trust them, I did try to do what I could to gain their trust to make my life a little bit easier. The communists turned people against each other to get people to tell on one another and then kill them when they told the truth. They wanted to kill people without wasting bullets. They would torture you until you killed yourself or killed another person. If you escaped, they would follow you. Like a tree, when they cut the branch, they would also cut the root. They would kill your family while they searched for you. When they found you, you would be killed, too.

With these facts in mind and following my escape attempt and close call with being executed, I did not want to give my captors any more reasons to make an example of me. I tried my hardest to be an exemplary prisoner. I made sure I only gave helpful suggestions. One example had to do with how I dealt with the camp guards who were mostly tribal men. These guards were Laotian, but they were from the mountain regions and part of tribes called "Kha" or "Akha." They were not lowland Lao people like the Hmong. People from the Kha tribe were poor, and they had no education. Communists preyed on and aggressively recruited poorly educated people. They thought these people did not know any better and that they would who follow orders with no questions asked. Communists did not like hard-headed people who asked a lot of questions. These guards did not even know what they were talking about when they called me and other prisoners "a dog CIA man." They were just parroting what the communists had taught them to say. They were taught to hate anyone having anything to do with the U.S. These guards were usually from 17 to 25 years old. They did not really understand the Lao language because they had their own language. Their limited background did prove to be helpful to me. These guards did not have cars and they did not know how to ride bikes, so they walked everywhere. I noticed that some of the cars and trucks stranded on the road after the war were still in good condition. I told these guards that those cars could be good and that I knew how to fix them. It helped that I had learned basic mechanics during my military training. Also, some of the broken-down cars had tools in the trunk. The Lao communists liked the idea of fixing the cars. I gathered some fellow prisoners; we worked on the car and made it drivable. We then fixed about 17 Chinese, Russian, and Vietnamese vehicles. I was recognized by my captors as being useful. I even received a certificate of recognition even though I was a prisoner. Meanwhile, I continued doing farm work for Colonel Khamdong, I would bring crops, like rice or potatoes, back to the camp to share with others.

Sometime later in 1978, Colonel Khamdong tipped me off that the Lao communists might want me to work on the airport that was being built with the help of the Russians in an area called Planofgar in the Xiangkhouang province. Apparently, the Lao communists previously began the construction themselves, building it by hand, just using human labor to lay out landing strips. The engineering was inferior because when an airplane tried to land, it almost crashed. The Lao communists then contacted the Russians to help assist to properly build the airport.

Colonel Khamdong was right, and the Lao communists approached me. They asked me what languages I spoke. I told them I spoke English, French and, of course, Laotian. I told them I knew how to drive and knew about mechanical things and engineering from my military training in Vientiane. I was then transferred to work on the construction crew that was building the airport.

When I began to help the Russians build the airport, I was still had shackles on my hands and legs. The Russian engineer I was assigned to was taken aback by my appearance in shackles and, through an interpreter, asked my guards why this was. The guards told the Russian engineer that I was a prisoner of war who had also worked for the CIA. Of course, I stayed silent about the accusation. The Russian engineer did not ask any more questions about my past in front of the guards. He asked me if I knew how to do certain things to help with building the airport, like drawing blueprints, cutting and clearing small trees and laying out the metal on the ground. I assured the Russian engineer I could do whatever was required.

During this time, I lived in a different area that was closer to the airport construction site but it was walking distance from Colonel Khamdong's house. I was still living in a hut house in a compound, but it was a little better than the hut in the concentration camp. The hut was big enough to house 50 men. Most of these men were not as skilled as me. They were mostly labor men who worked with machetes and shovels to assist the Russians. The bunks, which were long bamboo platforms that ran the length across the room, were raised two feet from the dirt floor. The bunk platforms were on both sides of the hut with a walkway in the middle. During the winter rainy season, dirt worms sought refuge in the hut and were found everywhere. It was an improvement from the concentration camp and the deep hole but a step down from the room I slept in at Colonel Khamdong's house. The hut was still guarded all day and all night, and it was in a locked and secured area.

The Russian engineer and I got along well and had a good relationship from the start. I knew how to draw the blueprints, so I assisted the Russian engineer with those and he appreciated my help. He would give me beer, candy, and cigarettes. I did not smoke or drink, but I made sure to put those items to very good use; I gave them to the Lao communist guards to make friends with them and gain their trust. I would get my meals from the Russians and if I did not like what I was served, I would also give it to the guards. The guards would ask me, "Why don't you eat it?" I said I just did not eat that kind of food or that I just wanted to share it with them. The Russian engineer noticed what I was doing, and he also asked me why I was giving my food to the guards. I repeated to him that I just did not eat that kind of food. The Russian engineer asked me what I would like to eat. Taken aback for a moment that I was being offered a choice, I asked for chicken. The Russian engineer told the Lao communists, using me to translate, to cook chicken and rice for me. From then on, I got to eat very well.

The Russian engineer had started using me as a supervisor, so I had more responsibility. The guards kept a close eye on me and followed me everywhere I went, even though I was in shackles. I took a risk and told the Russian engineer that I did not like the guards following me around because it made it difficult for me to concentrate on my work. I told the Russian engineer I could not complain about this to the guards, or they would kill me. However, if the Russian engineer communicated the problem to them, they would believe him because he was my boss. The Russian engineer did not speak the guards' tribal language, so he said to me, "Go ahead and tell them I said it was OK." I told the guards that the Russian engineer did not want them following me around all the time because it was hard for me to concentrate on the work. The guards said they would tell their boss. The Lao communist boss said, "OK, if the Russian man said not to follow him around, then don't follow him." In addition to being nice to the guards by giving them food, beer, and cigarettes, this was another step in keeping me off their radar.

I then had to work on getting rid of the shackles. I told the Russian engineer about the problem I had with the shackles; they were heavy, would damage my skin and cause infections. I asked the Russian engineer to tell the guards to uncuff and remove the shackles because they made it difficult to complete my work. I had to draw blueprints, use a machete and work inside the airplanes, and it made those tasks difficult. The Russian engineer agreed and, like before, told me to tell the guards that my boss was making this request. I told the guards that the Russian engineer now wanted the shackles removed so I could do my job better and be more productive. The guards did what the Russian engineer requested and removed the shackles from my hands and legs.

The only reason I believed these requests would be granted by the Lao communists was because I got along well with the Russian engineer. He saw I was a good person and a hard worker. I knew that I could now use the Russian engineer to get what I wanted. The Lao communists now knew that I always spoke for the Russian engineer so they would do what I asked.

Usually, the guards would sit far away from the prisoners during their breaks. But eventually, they started asking me to sit with them. At first, I refused. I told them, "I can't do that. If somebody sees me doing that, they will kill me." The guards said, "No, it's OK. You're our friend, you can sit with us." Little by little, I had succeeded in gaining their trust. However, when I was around them, they still had their guns within reach.

I had hoped that maybe I would hear some news from home since I was in a more open area. Unfortunately, where I was working was far from Vientiane and there were no visitors allowed in the area. Like they did for me, the guards did relax the shackle rule and allowed about 70 to 80 other prisoners to do their work without shackles on. At this point, the Russian engineer was giving me more supervisor-type work and I would help direct the other laborer prisoners to do whatever the engineer wanted done.

After about six months of working at the airport construction site, I was certain I had done a good job and was trusted by those I worked for. Bolstered by this confidence, I asked, and received permission from,

Colonel Khamdong to do some farming after I was done working on the airport. The only reason this was possible was the Lao communists knew how highly Colonel Khamdong thought of me. I was permitted to walk out from the prison area and go straight to his house. If I got there by dinner time, I could eat dinner with Colonel Khamdong and his family at their table. If I arrived after dinner time, he would save food for me.

Colonel Khamdong gave me supplies, seeds and empty land to farm. He trusted me and assured the Lao communists that I could be trusted. I would work at the airport until 4:00 p.m. then from 4:00 p.m. to 9:00 p.m. I would do farm work. During the first month, some guards would follow me and keep an eye on what I was doing. After that, they left me alone to work. These hours of farming were certainly a welcome break. I planted potatoes, yams, mustard, cauliflower, lettuce, and rice. When it was time to harvest, I would bring the crops back to the Colonel, the prisoners, the guards, and the kitchen. For this deed, I received more recognition certificates.

Sometimes Colonel Khamdong would go to the farm with me. We would have heart to heart talks. I told him that once the airport construction was completed, I wondered what would happen to me. I figured the Lao communists would transfer me somewhere to do something else. I also figured I would probably be a laborer and prisoner until I died. In 1980, during one of our visits on the farm, I asked Colonel Khamdong if it would be possible to go visit my family. He said he would try his best but the Lao communists would most likely not approve the visit. He repeated what he had told me before: dry my rice so if I ever "traveled" from here that I would have something to eat. That was his coded way of reminding me what I needed to do when I had a chance to escape. What that also meant was, whatever rice was left over from my meals each day, I should dry it out and save it so I could eat while traveling in the jungle. Most prisoners did not have enough rice to dry because the Lao communists only handed out a handful per meal. Fortunately, I not only got to eat at the prison, but I also got to eat at the Colonel Khamdong's house, so I had extra rice to save and dry.

During these visits with Colonel Khamdong, I also learned more about his background. His parents were killed and then he was placed in an orphanage in Laos. He was sent to Vietnam when he was nine years old and was raised as a communist. Colonel Khamdong explained to me, "When you are in their party, you have to be at the top level. If you are at the top, you will be treated well. But if you are at the bottom, you just get used by them and you will never be successful." Colonel Khamdong's position was at that lower level. I asked the Colonel if I, or any of the other prisoners would ever be released. Colonel Khamdong was blunt. "No way," he said. "They will never release you. You will die here someway, somehow. Either from working to death or they will kill you somehow. If you try to escape, you will be killed, or they will catch you and torture you until you kill yourself from depression or you will kill the other prisoners." These were hard words to hear but they confirmed what I thought was true. Colonel Khamdong went on to say, "The only way to stay alive is do your best and do whatever you need to do." If anybody in the Communist Party found out that Colonel Khamdong was talking to me like this, he would have been killed.

Colonel Khamdong went on to tell me a rumor that circulated around military circles about Prince Souphanouvong. He was the "red prince" who married a Vietnamese woman, and that woman was related to Ho Chi Minh. Souphanaouvong wanted to be a leader in Laos, and his older half-brother had been the Prime Minister of Laos. Colonel Khamdong told me that in 1969

Souphanouvong lived in a cave by the border of North Vietnam and Laos. He had even sent his older son to study in Moscow, Russia. When Souphanouvong's son returned to Laos, he realized the communists would use Souphanouvong's family for what they needed, and they would get rid of them later. He told his father that, "If we are going to be used only, we will never be what we wanted to be." Souphanouvong's son tried to sound out who had the same idea. Word got to the communists about the inquiries Souphanaouvong's son was making. The communists approached his father and mother and asked them, "Do you want to kill you son? Do you want to kill him, or do you want us to kill him? If you don't kill your son who questioned us, we will kill your whole family." Souphanouvong and his wife decided to have the communists kill their son, but they requested to see him die in front of them. Souphanouvong and his wife had no choice now. They had to show the communists that they were loyal to them without a shadow of a doubt.

Souphanaouvong and his wife prepared a good meal for their son. His mother prepared his favorite food. At the dinner table, after the son finished eating, the communists arrived and asked if dinner was all done. Souphanouvong nodded, then the communists shot his son. Colonel Khamdong told me this story to emphasize that there was no getting out. The communists would never trust me completely. "They will use you and they will get rid of you later on," he repeated. "Look at Souphanouvong and his brother. They are dead now." I asked Colonel Khamdong if he was worried about getting killed by the communists. Colonel Khamdong told me, "Do not worry about what will happen to me. You do what you need to do." I got the message loud and clear. What I needed to do was have the patience to wait for the right day to escape. I also decided that I would rather die trying to escape than spend the rest of my life waiting to be killed by the communists.

CHAPTER SEVENTEEN

By 1981, 70% of the airport construction had been completed. I began to think more seriously about escaping, especially after my many blunt talks with Colonel Khamdong. I continued to dry my rice and watched and waited for an opportunity. However, I realized that the odds were going to be against me. There were always guards inside the compound and guards outside the compound. I then realized that my problem was going to turn out to be my advantage. Since the time I arrived at the construction site in 1978, I had made efforts to befriend the guards and earn their trust. It got to the point that when I sat with the guards now, they would be lax with their guns and not keep them within arm's reach. A successful escape plan completely depended on the trust I had built up with the guards. I had become friendly with a certain crew of 14 guards. Since it was winter, those 14 guards would huddle around a bonfire to keep themselves warm. They would always ask me to join them so I could get a little warmth from the fire. They would let always let me do that because I was always giving them food, beer, and cigarettes. My plan began to take shape.

I knew I would need help to carry out my plan. I talked among my prisoner friends and asked them, "If the day comes when you can escape who would be willing to go and what would you be willing to do?" I had many friends who were willing to do whatever it took and whatever I asked. If we were able to escape, we then discussed signals we would need to use in the jungle to make sure we could identify each other in the likely event we got separated. We all knew there were five concentration camps around the country from north to south. Our camp was "Camp 3," and the code was "708." We agreed to use that code if we got separated and we needed to identify ourselves to meet again. For example, we would say, "Are you the seminar people? What is your code?" This would keep us from killing each other in the jungle.

Even though this plan to escape was my idea, I also wanted to help my fellow prisoners out of the camp. Everyone wanted to get out, they just needed the right opportunity. I believed I could give that to all of us. I also knew that even though Colonel Khamdong had looked out for me many times, I did not believe he would be able to protect me this time if I was caught. All he could do was advise me to try to save my life and he had already given me the nod to try to escape. I could not ask for or expect any more than that.

I told the other prisoners that they needed to be ready any time. "If you hear the gunshots, you need to be ready to go." The other prisoners were too weak and did not have the strength or mindset to make plans, so I wanted to make sure they saved their strength to just react and follow orders. I had gained strength to carry out this escape plan because I was able to eat better than most of the other prisoners. I ate from the farm, from Colonel Khamdong's house and I ate better food because I worked with the Russians. I had the strength to think clearly and plan carefully. Of course, I was worried someone might tell the communists what was going on. However, I was more concerned that if did not try to escape, I would die there.

Towards the end of March 1981, I determined that Tuesday, March 31 would be the day for the escape. I recall it was a Tuesday because I had heard the guards mention what day it was. I also recall this date because during my time working at airport, I had access to seeing a calendar due to my supervisory tasks. The camp I was assigned to was located at a high altitude, so it was cooler and foggier than the rest of the country. It also happened to be monsoon season. There were two rice plantings a year so around the time I planned the escape, the first rice planting happened so it must have been the end of March.

I had been observing the weather and it was still foggy and cold. Chances were that the guards would relax around the bonfire as they usually did during this time of year. I also knew that when they were looking at the bonfire and then turned away to look away at something else in the fog, their vision would be blurred. As a result of that blurred effect, they would not have time to clearly see what was going on around them. In other words, it was the perfect opportunity for me to get to their guns.

If the usual 14 guards were gathered around the bonfire, I needed to make sure there were more prisoners than guards to back me up after I carried out the first part of my plan. I told my fellow prisoners to get ready for the next day. As soon as the guards lit the bonfire, my men had to be ready. I also told the others that if everything went according to plan and we were able to escape, "We have to spread out, we cannot go in one direction. If we all go in one direction, the odds were that we would all be killed." It would be more difficult for the communists to track us down if we were spread out. The night before the escape, I prayed to my Master, the Buddha monk, to please protect me and the other prisoners because so we were making our escape tomorrow.

The next day, I was not convinced my Buddha Master had heard me. It started to warm up outside and I feared that if it got too warm, the guards would not start the bonfire. Fortunately, it did not get warm enough. When the Russian engineers left to eat, the 14 Lao communist guards gathered in their usual spot outside, sat in a circle and started the bonfire. I approached the guards like I usually did. The years and effort of befriending the guards certainly paid off. By this point, whenever I joined them, they trusted me enough that they stood their AK-47 guns up a few feet away from them. The guns were all grouped together in the shape of a teepee. None of these guards were ranked a captain or higher so I knew that none of them would have side arms or handguns. Despite this casual behavior by keeping their guns away from them, they kept bullets in their pockets and rounds of ammunition wrapped around their bodies. As I tended to do, I brought them cigarettes, beer and candy. As the guards enjoyed those things, they were completely relaxed. At that moment I knew my Buddha

Master had heard me. I felt like I had more power than I ever had, and I felt a tiger ready to attack. My body was trembling, too, but it was not out of fear.

Seeing how distracted the guards were, I knew it was now or never. I jumped up and grabbed an AK-47 from the group of guns nearby. As I suspected, because it was foggy, when the guards looked away from the bonfire, they could not make out what I was doing because their vision was blurred. I got on one knee. I pulled the trigger. Bullets flew. I shot the guard closest to me first. The other guards jumped to their feet They rushed towards me, instead of towards their guns. They figured I was just one man and the rest of them could stop me. They were wrong. I was able to shoot the rest of them with the machine gun rounds. With 30 bullets loaded into the AK-47, I was able to kill all 14 guards and I had bullets to spare. The sound of the shooting was the signal my men were waiting for. They rushed to the scene, and they grabbed the other guns and ammunition from the dead guards' jackets and pockets. We then all ran for our lives.

Even though the guards inside the compound were dead, there were still the guards outside the compound to deal with. Fortunately, the fog was excellent cover for us. Also, the chaos of what just happened made the other guards confused so we had a head start on them. When I escaped, I was not sure exactly how many other prisoners got out, too. It might have been between 70 and 80. I knew they all had military training, could use the weapons they had taken and could survive in the jungle. If they were not captured, they had a good chance to make it.

I recall being joined by 31 or 32 prisoners as we fled the compound. As I ran, I knew I had to do whatever it took to get back to Vientiane. Back in 1975 when I first was taken away to the concentration camp my mother was still there so that was where I was headed. We were hardly safe now by any measure. We knew that the communists would send out an alert by radio to the villages. The message would be that escapees from Camp 3 killed many soldiers and were armed with weapons. They would be warned that we were coming their way. If they saw us coming, they were instructed to kill us because we were very dangerous people. We had taken our first steps towards freedom. Yet the road to our destination was still long, risky, and uncertain.

CHAPTER EIGHTEEN

There are things one never forgets about war. One example would be the many paths that were traveled to and from the battles. As a result, when we made our escape that monumental day in 1981, we were all familiar with the area. We knew what direction to go by looking at the trees. If the side of the tree had thick bark, then that should be the east because of how the sun would hit it. We would go to the top of trees and hills to determine where we were exactly in the area. We also knew which places to avoid such as villages and roadways that were populated by the enemy.

In the daytime we traveled in the deep jungle. We avoided the villages. We knew every village was guarded by Lao communists and that the tribal guards would enjoy nothing more than capturing and killing us. In the nighttime we would walk on a dirt road. Sometimes we would nap briefly but mostly we walked day and night.

Out of necessity, we had to take food from farms. The rice I had saved over time and shared with my fellow escapees was not enough to keep us fed for long. I had instructed the men with me, "If you are going to eat something that belongs to someone else, you need to sit down, bow your head, and ask permission to get rice or food." As an example, I told them to say, "We are so hungry and please let us have some food to survive." We were not asking a person for this permission. Rather, we were asking Mother of Earth for food. We were making it known that we were not stealing but we were running for our lives and needed to survive. I told my men that if we had to sneak onto another's land and take food, we should eat just enough to survive. If we took a grain of rice, we made sure to suck the milk out of the rice. If we ate a cucumber, we ate the whole skin. The same went with stalks of corn. We did not want to leave remains or evidence that we were there. We certainly did not want the farmers to curse us or tip off the Lao communists.

During five or six nights we spent on foot, we passed through Sarachakhoun, Meuang Kasy, Meuang Vangvieng, Hinherb and Elimaka. We also traveled through Meuang Kham, Meuang Pak, Meuang Xieangkhouang, Meuang Ponesavanh, Paxamgnamjude (a river in Meuang Xui), and a towering mountain called Choulongjong. We finally reached a road we knew as Road #7. It was there that we heard footsteps in the forest, then people rushing around towards each other. I stopped, signaled my men to follow my lead, and then called out, "Are you seminar people?" The reply was, "Yes, Camp 3, 708." We were relieved to hear that answer and met up with nine other men who had escaped when we did. A few of them still had guns but the others did not. After some discussion with our fellow escapees, we figured out that close to 80 men had escaped but that some had been separated from their group or were killed.

Our new group kept walking. We had encountered no problems or sights of the enemy. So far, so good. Early one morning, between 4 or 5 a.m., we approached a rice field near a village called Ban Nahoy in the Xieangkhouamg province. We were startled by gunfire. We were clearly the target. Our luck had run out; the Lao communists had us in their sights. I ordered my men to stay down. "When they stop shooting," I said, "We have to make it to the rice field." The rice field offered us good coverage to escape if we were careful getting there. While the enemy was still shooting, three of my men got up and ran. I yelled at them to stay down and to crawl slowly. These three men refused to listen to me, and they were riddled with bullets. While our hope and strength were not good, five of us still had our weapons and some ammunition left. We fired back at the enemy, gave ourselves enough cover and time to barely escape.

After escaping that attack, we traveled as fast as we could to a big river called Nam Jue. The water levels were very high, and the rapids were dangerous because it was monsoon season. Fearing that the Lao communists were in fast pursuit of us, we knew we had no choice but to cross that river. What made the crossing even more dangerous was that even if we made it to the other side, there was a communist military base nearby. To avoid running into more enemy soldiers, we traveled up the riverbank a good distance before entering the water. From this position, we would reach a mountainous area on the other side of the river which was far enough away from the military base. It was an even more dangerous crossing than I imagined. Despite my strong swimming skills, the strong currents had their way with me. Many of my fellow escapees almost drowned during the crossing because their strength had been sapped due to our strenuous journey

Somehow, we all managed to get to the other side of the river. We were even more exhausted than before. However, there was no time to rest. We now had to climb the mountain and cross over it to avoid the Lao communists. It took about three days to go from one side of the mountain to the other side. We still could not afford to take too much time to rest. It was a great risk just to steal short naps while leaning against the trees. Adding to our discomfort, we were walking with no shoes. Our feet were aching from stepping on thorns and rough terrain. We generally had scratches all over our bodies. Of course, in many of the areas we passed through, there were always leeches that attached to us and sucked our blood. This time, we had no diesel fuel to keep them off our bodies. There was nothing easy about our 18-day journey.

By the time we were approaching the border of Vientiane, there were only three of us traveling together. I still had my gun with only a few bullets left. As we headed towards a farm, I overheard some people approaching and talking. We could not assume anybody was friendly by this point. I was prepared to kill these people if they turned out to be Lao communist guards. We took cover on the ground by some bushes. My hand was on the trigger, ready to shoot. The people approaching the farm came into clear view; they were a family, a father, mother, and their child. I came very close to killing them.

After the family passed, the other two men and I walked for another kilometer or so. We were very close to

Vientiane. It dawned on me that the gun I was carrying was a Russian gun. It would be a terrible idea to come home carrying a gun from the enemy. Using the sharp point of the gun, I dug a hole about a foot deep and buried the gun and bullets in the bushes. The two other prisoners and I then said goodbye to each other. We wished each other well and we hoped that we would all be able to see our families again. One man walked off to the north, the other man went south, and I headed to straight to Vientiane. It was hard to believe but I was almost home.

There is that saying that you can never truly go home again. It did not take me long to see that this was true. When I finally got to Vientiane in the afternoon, I did not go into the village right away because of how I looked. I was filthy, had a wild beard and long hair that went down to the small of my back. I looked too different from everybody else. I stayed hidden in the fields and waited until it was dark. I then went to my parents' old house. The door was locked. Upon closer inspection, it looked like the communists had taken over the place and turned it into a government building. My family had other houses, so I went to another one to see if any family members were still there. People in Laos do not usually move around much because relatives stay in other family members' houses if that family member leaves. I went to see a cousin on my mother's side who lived in one of the other houses. I knocked on the door and told them who I was. My cousin recognized my voice and opened the door. Shocked as he was to see the sight of me, he let me inside right away. When I went inside the house, everyone there cried. They confirmed what I had thought, that my father was also sent to a concentration camp. They did not know if he was alive or not. They also told me my mother thought I was dead and that she had a funeral for me. I asked them where my mother was. They said that she had moved to the old capital of Luang Prabang sometime in 1976. Now I at least knew where to find one of my parents and that she was alive.

My cousins wanted to know how I escaped. There were so many other people who were in concentration camps who had not come home so they must have died. After telling them how I escaped, the family wanted to give me sticky rice to eat, figuring I would be very hungry. I had learned in the military that when you were very hungry, you could not fill up on heavy food like sticky rice. I instead asked for rice soup because eating too much on a shrunken stomach could have killed me. I also asked to shave and to take a shower. The family helped me shave because I was too exhausted to do it myself. They sat me down and shaved my eyebrows, face, hair, and body. One of my cousins said to me, "From now on all of the bad and evil things that have happened to you are gone. You are re-born, and you are a new person." After my family gave me that blessing, I took a shower. I was so happy because for the first time in many, many years I got my hand on green soap. Even though this kind of soap was used for the dishes, I used it to wash myself and it smelled so good.

After I cleaned myself, I felt like a new person indeed. I then sat down to eat. My family looked at my feet. There were imbedded thorns, cuts, scratches all over them. I did not feel anything, though, because my feet had become used to the pain. My cousin used pilers to pull the thorns out of my feet. Now my feet were bleeding, but it did not bother me. I had been through much worse.

Once I was full of good rice soup, I collapsed in a real bed and slept for almost two nights straight. I woke up briefly to eat a little something but then I just went back to sleep. While I slept my cousin went out to get me new clothes. My third day back in civilization was the day

I went to look for my girlfriend. On the way to her house, I finally took a good look around Vientiane. I hardly recognized it. The city had changed for the worse under communist rule. It was now an empty city, like a ghost town. No one was walking around, there were no cars, there were no businesses open. The big car dealership was empty. People were escaping the city every day.

When I arrived at where my girlfriend had lived, the big house was empty. I asked an old man who was their neighbor where my girlfriend and her family were. The old man was quiet for a moment before he pointed to the Mekong River nearby. The old man told me that her family paid two men to take them in a boat over to Thailand to escape the communist rule in Vientiane. One man sat in the front of the boat and the other was in the back to paddle. As they crossed the Mekong, and they were spotted by Lao communist guards. The communists opened fire on the boat. My girlfriend, her younger brother and parents dove in the water. When my girlfriend's younger brother made it across the river to Thailand, he looked for the rest of his family. There was no sight of them. My girlfriend and her parents were either shot in the water or drowned before they reached the Thailand shore.

I had been able to endure many horrible things while fighting on the battlefield and being held as a prisoner in a concentration camp. Having to endure this latest horror was too much to handle. I made my way to the riverbank of the Mekong, fell to my knees, and broke down. I cried out loud to my girlfriend, "I promised you I would come back but I'm here too late." I sat there for a long time. I thought about what war did to people, what corrupt governments did when they only acted is in their own interests and did not truly consider the people. I once had everything: a family, a girlfriend, a country. I never thought the day would come where I would have lost it all.

CHAPTER NINETEEN

On my fourth day back in Vientiane, my cousin gave me money to travel to Luang Prabang so I could find my mother. I packed two to three outfits that my cousin got me in a backpack. My cousin also told me there would be three checkpoints between Vientiane and Luang Prabang. One was near the area where I had buried my gun, the second checkpoint was at Saraprakhoun and the last one was at the first bridge before entering Luang Prabang.

I caught my first ride for the beginning leg of the trip with a cargo truck that carried supplies back and forth. When we got close to the checkpoint, I asked the driver to please stop the truck. When the truck stopped, I would get out to avoid being spotted by the Lao communist guards. I then had to traverse a lot of deep rolling hills. I would go down to the bottom of the hill and walk along the riverbank. Many times, the hills were so steep I would fall down the hill and get dirty. After I passed the checkpoint area, I would climb up the hill again. I would resume walking along the road, waiting for an opportunity to catch a ride with another cargo truck. I continued doing that routine until I got past the first bridge checkpoint area at Luang Prabang, which happened at around four in the morning.

After I got out of the cargo truck I headed over to my grandfather's big white house. I was confident that some family member would be living there. I walked past the bakery in town. They had just started baking their bread. It smelled so good! When I arrived at my grandfather's house, I knocked on the door. The person who answered the door was my older half-brother, Thao Yai. Despite Thao Yai's difficult personality, I thought we had a civil relationship. Before the communists took over, Thao Yai had his own clothing and sports supply business. Thao Yai had been supported by our father until he was taken away by the communists. Despite no longer having the financial support of my father, Thao Yai was making a comfortable living. As soon as Thao Yai realized it was me at the door, he said, "You have to go, you have to go, I can't let you in the house." Thao Yai was now the head of the village and if the communists discovered that I was there, he claimed they would kill us both. I told Thao Yai, "I have been walking for 18 hours without food. Can you at least buy me some bread to eat? I'm very hungry from my journey." My money had run out because I used it all to pay the cargo truck drivers who had given me the rides to Luang Prabang. Thao Yai could not be bothered with me and again told me to leave. He would not even give me any water or rice. He repeated that he was afraid he would be killed if the communists found out I was even talking to him. I could not believe what he was saying to me. I asked Thao Yai, "Who is going to tell if you don't tell them? It's just you and me." His response was to go to my mother's farmhouse in Luang Prabang. He then turned his back on me, walked into the house and shut the door. I was speechless and very sad by him turning his back on me. I thought that because we had the same father he would put aside whatever differences he had with me. I was wrong.

There was nothing left to do but keep traveling on to my mother's house. She was staying in a farmhouse about four hours away by foot. I finally arrived at the farmhouse at about 8:00 a.m. Usually, according to the customs in Buddhism, the local monk comes around at that time, carrying an empty black rice bowl. The monk passed by people's houses and the people would give him something to eat. My mom offered food to the monk that morning, and when she came back to the farmhouse, I was waiting. When I called for her, she stared at me from the window. She was either in shock or she did not recognize me at all. Either way, I could not blame her because I probably weighed 100 pounds. My mother looked very different to me, too. She had grown very old and thin. She kept asking me, "Who are you?" I kept saying, "This is me, Mom. I'm your son." It finally dawned on my mother what was happening. She dashed out from the house and we both cried. My younger brother and sister joined us, too, and we all cried. My mother wasted no time cooking chicken soup for me. I was so happy and overwhelmed that I could only eat a little bit. I then walked out of the farmhouse to fulfill the wish that I had when I was a prisoner. My mother, sister, and brother watched as I climbed up a tree and grabbed a coconut for them.

We finally spent some time talking about what had happened to each of us during those many years apart. My mother told me she thought I was never coming back, and she thought I had died a long time ago. When my father and I left Vientiane in 1975, she was suddenly a single mother with five young children to look after. Her situation was very bad because she had no money and no support from the government. Her relatives who were part of the Royal Family were taken away to the concentration camps. She soon realized that the communists lied by saying they were taking certain people to a "seminar" to teach them learn the new ways of communists. As the rumors of communists killing off members of royal families and high-ranking military officers circulated in Vientiane, my mother also presumed my father was dead because he was a general. She then told me a story that surprised me. My mother had heard a rumor that people in the concentration camp were blown up and that I could have been in that group. She thought I had died so she had a funeral for me. My mind raced back to that incident where the bonfire had caused an undetonated U.S. bomb to explode. I recalled that I did not feel hungry for three days. It turned out the reason for that was because of a Buddhism belief. When there is a funeral service, food is offered to the Buddha monk who is a conduit to bring food to the spirit of the dead person. During the funeral service the Buddha monk said if I was in the spirit world then my spirit would receive what my mother sent; if I was hungry, then I would be full.

The information about that bombing reached my mother because the communist military men who traveled and brought things into the villages and cities had heard about it. Word would then spread throughout the local community. When my mother heard the news about me possibly being killed in the explosion, she was grief-stricken. Despite her devastation, she did not ask any questions because that would raise suspicion among the communists. She also did not want to give away that she knew I was being held prisoner in a camp. I was using a fake name (my mother's maiden last name) so any revelation that I was in the camp would have meant death to me. No one could trust anybody during this time. It was common for the communists to have spies hiding under people's houses or linger nearby to eavesdrop on people's conversations. After learning about the bombing, my mother never heard any more news about me or my father.

Once the communists took over, my mother had to let her servants, drivers, and security guards go. She had to sell all her property and cars for a loss to people who still had money. She sold her jewelry and other valuables. A general's wife's silk outfits were very valuable, so she sold those, too. After she sold everything, the communist party took over a couple of houses that belonged to our family. Those properties were turned into government offices. When my mother ran out of money, she took my other siblings back to Luang Prabang. Her remaining family there felt sorry for her. She told them what happened to her family. They gave her many bags of rice grain. about 400kgs (or 200lbs) worth. She took ten bags of rice and sold them to buy other necessities. When my mother had nothing to sell, she would trade and barter for things. That is how she came to live in the old farmhouse. She had to do farm and field work to live there. Survival was still not a guarantee. Two of my siblings became very sick and they died because of malaria. My mother fell into a depression. How many more family members would she lose? Her parents had already passed away. She thought of committing suicide many times but if she was gone there would be no one left to take care of her surviving children. The communists knew where my mother lived. She was not a threat to them, though, because she had no weapons. The communists would still patrol the village and would eavesdrop on conversations. My mother just tried to stay inconspicuous. Despite everything that was happening, my mother, like other women in Laos at that time, had no political voice. Her job used to be a housewife. Now she had to keep what family she had left alive, so she focused on that and did not think much about what was going on politically.

After I reunited with my family for a little while, I took a much-needed nap. When I woke up, I walked into the city and looked for a job. I wanted to help bring money to my family as soon as possible. There was a large river in the city where ferry boats would travel up and down, carrying supplies, such as rice, household supplies, and cement. I found a job on one of those boats helping to load and unload the cargo. The hours were long and the work back-breaking, conditions I was well used to. I would work 16-hour days. I would carry 100-pound cement bags on my back from the boat to a delivery truck. The bags had been handled and tossed around many times before it got to me, so there would be rips in the bags. As a result, cement would leak out and burn my back. The only remedy for the burns was to soak myself in the water. Often the burns would be so severe that they would blister. I tried wrapping a cotton towel around my shoulders when I carried the cement bags but that offered little protection. I also made sure to wear a hat so no one would recognize me. I was still a fugitive, after all. I earned 700 kip which was about $30 for a day's work. Every day I would show up at the ferry boat docks and I got steady work because others did not want to do what I was doing. I did not mind the hazardous work because I was able to help my family. I worked every day on the docks for about four months. During this time, I stayed with my mother and siblings in the farmhouse. I also was aware that more and more people were fleeing Laos to get away from the communists.

Now that I was home, my mother told me I had to become a Buddha monk. She had prayed to Buddha, "If my son comes home, I will have him become a Buddha monk for you." She made the same prayer for my father. I went to prepare to be a monk. My Master for this training was an Auprarach which meant "king of the Buddha." This Master's name was Chao Auprarach Sisavangvong, he was from a royal family, and he was head of the monks throughout Laos. Master Sisavangvong and my mother knew each other, and he also knew my entire family. He also knew the king and his family had been killed in the concentration camp.

During the week I lived with and trained with Master Sisavangvong, he taught me many things and we had many close conversations. He told me, "Do not forget the one who has grace to you. Do not envy and crush someone who is rich or someone because of their merit. You are a good man to survive the hell on earth." He taught me that if I left Laos, I had to make sure to go all the way to a "third world country." He instructed me not to stay by the border, and not to try to come back until I was ready. Master Sisavangvong knew he may also have to leave Laos when the time came. The communists were going around to the Buddha temples, piling up the religious books and treasures in front of the temple and burning them. They had burned books written on ancient palm leaves. Attempts were made to save these ancient books and hide them in wood boxes in the caves. Master Sisavangvong knew the communists did not believe in any religion. He feared they would destroy Buddhism.

Master Sisavangvong taught me advanced meditation techniques. He showed me the first meditation position where one sits down, left leg over right leg, right hand over left hand, two thumbs touching each other, to be followed with deep breathing. He also showed me a second position: palms down on both legs, then changing to palms up if the body got numb. Overall, he emphasized how the mind could truly control the body.

During my training, I contemplated what I wanted to do for the rest of my life. Carrying the cement down at the docks was a very hazardous job. I knew I had other skills which would lend themselves to finding better work, but it was not an easy thing to do. I had been gone from civilization for a long time. The communists had wiped out the old system. There was also the sensitive matter about my identity. There was paperwork to certify that a person was part of the village one lived in. I had no paperwork to document who I was. Fortunately, I had an uncle who was a successful goldsmith and he promised to help me establish a new identity. He recognized me when I returned home because my walk looked familiar to him. He could not believe I had survived and escaped from the camp. He was happy to help me. He picked a new name for me and came up with a way to add me as part of his household. "This is my cousin from Vientiane," my uncle would say. "Now he lives here in Luang Prabang." There was no way to disprove what my uncle said. Official documents from the old government had been destroyed once the communists took over. There was no need for a birth certificate, drivers' license, or any other kind of identification. The authorities just wanted to know who the primary head of the household and who his family members were. To make sure things went smoothly, my uncle bribed officials not to ask any follow up questions. Once my uncle registered the members of his household, it was certified by head of the village. After that happened, I received a piece of paper that stated I was who my uncle said I was and that I was a resident in the village.

In 1982, while I kept working and saving some money, I thought of other things to do for work. I thought of the days when I was a boy, and I helped my grandfather with different tasks in his medical practice. I also thought about all the medical techniques I mastered during my military training. I had a good idea now what to do next. I took some money I had saved and went to the pharmacy. In those days, a pharmacist did not need a license and a person did not need a prescription to buy medicine. I knew about different medications and how to administer them. Malaria was a common disease that afflicted people in the area. Quinine was used to treat malaria. I bought a lot of quinine as well as other medications for pain. I bought syringes and an intravenous apparatus. I carried those medications in my backpack and walked to the village that was two to three hours away from Luang Prabang. Those people had no healthcare or doctors there. I discussed my services with head of the village. He was very happy to have medical help. Of course, no one from the communist government had ever come to help them. The villagers suffered from a lot of fevers and malaria. I now provided basic medical services to these villagers. I promised that I would come by every week to treat them. For my services I asked to be paid five silver coins. However, I never forgot what my grandfather had done for those who could not afford to pay for his services. I followed my grandfather's example. If the people I treated did not have money, it would be no problem and they could give me whatever they were able to give. I branched out and traveled up north to other villages to offer my medical services.

After being back with my family for a while, I finally revealed to my uncle how my half-brother Thao Yai had treated me when I arrived at my grandfather's house. My uncle was not happy about this at all. He went to Thao Yai's house and asked him why he had treated me so disrespectfully. "Why were you so mean to your brother?" my uncle demanded to know. "You had no right to do that." My uncle reminded Thao Yai that because his mother committed adultery and was divorced from our father, by law, Thao Yai had no right to the house. Thao Yai lied to the face of my uncle and said he did offer to help me. My uncle told me to move into the big house. Thao Yai had no legal rights, and he would be forced out eventually. I decided to not bother with Thao Yai and I let him stay there with his own family. I was single, I did not need such a large house, and I was not sure what the future held for me in Vientiane. Even though I was making better money, I gave most of it to my mother. After all I had been through, I decided I was not ready for marriage, anyway. Life had other plans for me, though.

CHAPTER TWENTY

In 1982, a local man named Captain Pao was getting married. He was a former fellow prisoner who had escaped from a concentration camp before I did. Two or three of Captain Pao's friends asked me to help collect money to buy some pigs to slaughter for the wedding meal. I also volunteered to bring coconuts from my mother's farm to use for cooking the wedding meal. Older coconuts were used for cooking, and the younger coconuts were used for dessert and juice. Captain Pao's house was near the Mekong River. The distance between his house and my mother's farmhouse was about 7 or 8 kilometers. I pushed a two-wheeled cart filled with the coconuts all the way to his house, and I worked all day to deliver three loads of coconuts. I also used a black barrel to collect eight barrels of water from the Mekong River for the guests to drink. My hard work caught the eye of a royal family who lived nearby. The princess of the family was 24 years old and very attractive. Princess Phonesiri was tall, slim and wore her hair in a bun like other royal Lao women did. She watched me carry the coconuts and the water up and down the riverbank, was impressed with my hard work and asked Captain Pao, "Who is that person?" Captain Pao informed her, "Your Highness, he is the nephew of the goldsmith man." My uncle was a respected man in the city because he was one of the sons of my grandfather. It was because of my well to do pedigree that Phonesiri could not believe that I was a laborer. Phonesiri's mother was also impressed with my work ethic, and she was interested in having me meet her daughter.

When Captain Pao told me a young woman was interested in me. I did not say anything because I was still mourning the death of my girlfriend. I was also not happy that I was poor. I wanted to build myself back up before I settled down with anyone. I simply was not ready for marriage.

One day, as I walked past Phonesiri's house, she appeared and called me in. I entered the house and kneeled when talking to her because that was the custom when visiting a royal family. Even though I technically was from a royal family, too, I still observed the custom. Phonesiri asked me, "Are you related to the goldsmith man?" Based on the modest way I dressed and the way I worked as a laborer made her think that perhaps I was adopted and not blood related to my uncle's family. I told her I was indeed related to my uncle. That was all Phonesiri wanted to know for the time being.

On Captain Pao's wedding day, I was helping getting things ready. Unbeknownst to me, Captain Pao invited my uncle to attend the wedding ceremony. He even gave my uncle a VIP seat so that he could sit far away from the other guests. Phonesiri's mother saw me and said, "We are talking about you." She then walked over to my uncle, kneeled in front of him because he was higher class than her and asked him, "I want to know who that young man is." My uncle replied, "That is my flesh and blood nephew." Nobody other than my uncle knew that I escaped the concentration camp. Phonesiri's mother told my uncle that she had a daughter. An understanding was to set up between the two of them. My uncle said to Phonesiri's mother, "If you really like my nephew you need to come and see me after the wedding."

Even though she was from royalty, Phonesiri worked in the capitol as the deputy governor. She happened to work with my half-brother Thao Yai and she was his boss. Two weeks after Captain Pao's wedding, Phonesiri and her mother paid me a surprise visit at my mother's farmhouse. At the time, I was cutting sugar cane that I had planted. I would cut the stalks, put them in a two-wheeled cart and took the crops to the market to sell them. When Phonesiri and her mother arrived, her mother asked me, "Oh, are you doing farm work?" I replied, "Yes, this is how I make my living. I plant sugar cane and banana leaves, I cut them, and I sell them at the market." I told them I also farmed potatoes, yams, and rice. Phonesiri's mother said, "Now that I know you are the nephew of the goldsmith man, I want to take you to your uncle's house so we can talk." I already had a good idea what they were going to talk about. To my surprise, Phonesiri said, "I can help you with the sugar cane, I know how to do that." She then helped me cut the sugar cane stalks and tie them in bundles. She showed me it was not beneath her to do this work and she ever joked it was an easy job. It let me know that Phonesiri really liked me. I was afraid she would cut herself because there were little hairs on the sugar cane stalks that could poke one's fingers. I kept saying she was going to hurt herself, but she insisted she could do it. I was very impressed with Phonesiri.

Phonesiri asked me to stop working for a little bit so we could go to my uncle's house. While I really did not want to go, and I did not think I was ready for marriage, I agreed to go. When we arrived at my uncle's house, I took one look at my uncle and Phonesiri's mother and I already knew what the deal was going to be. I said in front of all of them, "Uncle, I do not want to settle down with anybody yet. I have to build myself first. I am poor and if I have a wife what am I going to do? How am I going to survive? Let me make some money and save. When I am ready to have a wife, I'll let you know." I had a lot of pride and my uncle kindly let me speak my mind. No sooner did I stop talking my uncle brushed aside what I had just said and assured me, "It's OK, I will take care of everything for you. I feel bad I couldn't help you in the past. I will make it up to you now." Money was not a worry for my uncle. He was the only goldsmith in town. My uncle asked Phonesiri's mother, "If you are OK for them to marry, how much will you ask for?" In Lao culture, the groom's family had to pay a dowry to the bride's family. Depending on how wealthy the bride's family was, they must be in the same class as the groom's family. Royalty usually married royalty, or the groom must be of a higher class than the bride. Phonesiri was pretty, and a lot of men wanted to marry her. Phonesiri's father was also in favor of me marrying his daughter, but he allowed his wife to take care of the arrangement. Phonesiri's mother suggested that the dowry would be 10 ounces of gold in the form of a necklace or a bracelet. The value of such items was 10,000 baht or around $10,000. I did not have that kind of money and I did not want to owe money to anybody. My uncle again insisted I never had to pay him back and that he just wanted to help me. It was no use arguing with him.

My uncle went ahead and made plans for the wedding. Meanwhile, Phonesiri's mother requested that my uncle put the dowry on a tray to show everybody during the engagement. Her family did not want to give the impression that they gave away their daughter for nothing. However, after everyone had seen the dowry on display, Phonesiri's family returned it to my uncle. I did not believe this had happened at first. Phonesiri confirmed this had indeed happened. She only wanted me, and she did not want the dowry. She was truly a good person.

During the pre-wedding preparations, the rumor about the dowry being returned to my uncle had somehow reached my half-brother Thao Yai. Thao Yai went to Phonesiri who was his boss at work, and he told her, "You know, there are a lot of people who like you and there are people with more qualifications than who you are going to marry. He isn't even my blood related brother. He just came from the concentration camp, and he does not have anything. Why did you pick him, anyway?" Phonesiri relayed what Thao Yai had said to her mother. They then came to talk to me. I was not comfortable with what Thao Yai had told Phonesiri. I told her, "If you believe my half-brother at all let's stop at this point." Phonesiri assured me that she knew Thao Yai was jealous and a liar. She still wanted to be with me.

After learning what Thao Yai had said about me, I went to my uncle and told him the story. My uncle was furious. He ordered Thao Yai to come and see him at once. When Thao Yai stood before my uncle, he stood there in fear. Thao Yai tried to explain that he made a mistake in what he said and that those words just "spit out of his mouth." My uncle told Thao Yai, "You can't do that to your brother. He hasn't done anything to harm you. This is you trying to destroy him. You are just jealous, and you are a coward." My uncle did not stop there. He also threatened Thao Yai again by reminding him that I had legal rights to the house Thao Yai was living in with his family. My uncle said, "If my good nephew wants to move into that house you will have to move out." Thao Yai's big mouth also got him into bigger trouble. Phonesiri confronted Thao Yai at work. She told him, "You are such a liar and a bad person. I don't want even to talk to you again." As Thao Yai's boss, she made sure he was transferred out of his job at the capitol.

The marriage between Phonesiri and I took place in early 1983. Even though we tried to let bygones be bygones and invited Thao Yai to the wedding, he did not show up. This was a big royal wedding which required traditional silk outfits and a lot of gold chains. At dinner time, I changed into a suit. It was certainly nice to celebrate such a happy occasion after so many years of wondering if I would ever know happiness again.

After our wedding, my wife helped me get a job in her department in the capitol. My new job was to collect property taxes and business taxes for the province. In 1984, we welcomed the birth of our son. My mother-in-law had asked if the baby could have her last name, which was also the King's last name. However, I knew that communists still wanted to get rid of anything and anyone related to royalty, so out of caution I declined to use that name. Phonesiri and I ended up naming our son after Kelly, my girlfriend who had been killed. For the first time in a long time, I felt some sense of peace. It was not to last.

CHAPTER TWENTY-ONE

I thought my troubles with Thao Yai were over. He
had been transferred and demoted by my wife because of
what he had said about me. However, when Thao Yai
learned that I now had a better job than him, he grew
even more jealous. He was also fearful that I would one
day take back my grandfather's house from him. Towards
the end of 1984, Thao Yai went to his new workplace and
asked to talk to his boss, a man named General Keo. He
told General Keo that I had escaped from a concentration
camp. What Thao Yai did not know was that I worked
with General Keo before I was sent to the concentration
camp.

General Keo came to see me that very day. He told
me that Thao Yai was telling people that I was trying to
gather people to go against the communist party. He told
me that because of what Thao Yai was saying I needed to
flee right away. My mind raced. I wondered for a moment
if Thao Yai was a communist. I then thought probably not.
He was just greedy, petty, and jealous. Thao Yai had not
been able to get into the Air Force even though our father
was high up in the military. His older brother had died in
battle and was a national hero. I had served my country

honorably. Thao Yai probably could not stand the thought of me ever doing better than him. Yet his insecurities were now threatening my life and the lives of my family. General Keo warned me that if I did not leave Laos, the communists would pick me up the next morning and it would not go well for me after that. He tried to assure me that they were just coming for me and that no harm would come to my wife and son. I knew that if the communists took me this time, they would slice up my body, put salt on the wounds and just wait until I died.

There was no other option for me but to leave. My wife now had to decide what to do. She could not bring herself to leave her parents and our son was only a few months old. My wife's parents were wealthy and owned a lot of land. They asked my wife to wait until they died and then she could go to be with me. Unfortunately for me there was no time for waiting. My wife's parents did not know the full extent of my experience in the camps and that I was a wanted man because of my escape. I had to leave the country right away. I packed whatever I could, as fast as I could, in a military backpack. General Keo gave me some money, all of it in Thai currency. I then went to say goodbye to my mother, brother, and sister. My mother gave me two ounces of gold. She wanted to give me all the money she had but I refused. I said I would use the money that General Keo gave me. We all cried. It was not long ago we had just cried because I had been reunited with them. I told my family I would try my best to survive again.

I left Luang Prabang in the evening and began the all-night journey that would take me to Vientiane. I had to do exactly what I did to get to Luang Prabang after my first escape: alternate between traversing the hills to avoid checkpoints and catching rides with cargo trucks once I was clear of the checkpoints. The word was out that I was a wanted man so the checkpoints would be looking out for me. As I walked and caught rides with cargo trucks, so many thoughts raced through my mind. I could not believe I had to leave my family again. Would I ever see them again? Would they be safe? Could I make it safely across the Mekong River to Thailand? What would my life be like even if I could even get to Thailand? The past haunted me, and my present and future were equally scary to think about. I risked my life to escape to get home once. Now I had to risk it again to escape from home.

I arrived in Vientiane the next afternoon. I now had to figure out how to cross the narrow but dangerous

Mekong River. I decided to make a floating device and to leave from a different shore that was not as heavily patrolled by the communists. The haunting images of my girlfriend and her parents' death during their crossing were still fresh in my mind. I chose to depart from the shore located near a village called Nongda. I cut the trunks of two banana trees and tied them together with rope to make a flotation device. I watched and waited until I was sure there were no guards around to spot me. Not that I needed the reminder, but I kept in mind the fact that many tried to escape to Thailand, and many died before reaching their destination. My strategy was to do everything I could to cross safely. The shore at Nongda was a good bet; the water was not that high, and it was the narrowest and shortest crossing. I decided to put my clothes in my backpack and only wear underwear in the water. I finally waded into the very cold river with my homemade raft. I laid on top of the raft like a surfboard and started kicking and paddling. It was quiet when I started crossing the river. I was afraid the guards would spot me at any moment and start shooting. So far, though, my journey across the Mekong was undetected. I continued putting distance between myself and Laos when the banana trunk raft hit a rock in the middle of the river. The force of the collision flipped over the raft and threw me in the water. The raft got away from me. I swam in the cold and strong current, unable to see much around me. It was exhausting and, despite my strong swimming skills, I thought I might drown. Somehow, during my treacherous swim in the water, I bumped into the raft again. I climbed back on it and paddled the rest of the way as fast as I could. I do not know how long it took me to cross the Mekong River that night. It felt like it took forever. Yet sometime after midnight, I finally made it to shore in Thailand.

Safe for the moment in Thailand, I took my clothes out of backpack and even though they were soaking wet from the crossing, got dressed again. I thought about my next steps. There was not much I could do until morning, so I took a nap. At sunrise, I awoke and started walking, not exactly sure where I was going. I had no contact with the CIA after U.S. forces and personnel left Laos back in 1975. I thought of going to the U.S. Embassy in Bangkok to contact the CIA, but that city was far away, and I was not familiar enough with how to navigate in this new country. I soon arrived at a house. I knocked on the door. A local man answered, and I explained that I had just crossed the Mekong River and why I had done so. This man seemed to understand my situation very well. The local Thai people were familiar with people escaping from Laos and asking them for help daily. The man told me to go to the police station and talk to them. He directed me to the station which was about an hour away by foot.

When I arrived at the police station, I approached a police captain named Aumpai who was around my age. I showed him a small military picture of myself that my mother had given me. The police in Thailand were aware that some people from Laos escaped from concentration camps or some were escaping the horrible way of life imposed by the communists. The police in the area were also military men. Aumpai and his fellow officer were welcoming, told me I was lucky to have made it across the Mekong and asked me to tell them the entire story of my escape. They also brought in some news reporters from Bangkok to interview me. I gave the reporters a fake name, told them the details about the concentration camp and about my escape. The reporters asked if I was in the military and about my knowledge of guns. They gave me an AK-47, an M-16, a .45 handgun and asked me to take them apart and put them back together again to prove I was in the military. Of course, I could literally do such tasks with my eyes closed.

Aumpai treated me very well. He asked me if I had any money. I had used all the money that was given to me by General Keo so I replied that all I had were the clothes on my back and my military picture. Aumpai reached into his pocket and handed me about 1500 baht. He drove me in his jeep to town to buy some new clothes and treated me to dinner. He then took me to one of the military houses so I could get some sleep.

I returned to the police station to get my paperwork processed so I would be officially classified as a refugee. When my paperwork was processed, Aumpai took me to the Napho refugee camp where I met with the head of the camp. Fortunately, they had room in a house for me because some other refugees had just left for another country. The houses in the camp were temporary shelters built out of bamboo. These structures were also easy to burn down. During the year that I stayed in the camp, the communists would send people to burn down these houses. The communists would pretend to be refugees, enter the camps, and then sabotage them. A lot of the buildings in the camp were burned down. One of these attacks happened after I saw three men come towards me. I recognized they were communists because one of the men was Khamphet, also known as Phet, who was one of the guards at the concentration camp I was a prisoner at. I called out the name "Phet! Phet!" He and his comrades knew I was on to them. People in the refugee camp chased after them but they had already started a fire that burned down a lot of houses.

Refugees were not Thai citizens so all we had was what the refugee camp gave us. For example, children of refugees were not allowed to go to Thai schools. However, we could leave the camp for periods of time. We were given an identification card so in the event we were stopped by authorities or the police we could show them we were refugees. The camp also provided transportation in the form of a small car that would take us wherever we wanted to go. The only restriction was that if we wanted to leave the province, we had to let the camp know exactly where we were going and for how long.

Once I got settled into the refugee camp, I heard there was a resident Buddha Master who was offering training like my other Buddha Masters had done. I went to see the refugee camp Buddha master and asked him for a tattoo to further protect me in the future. That Buddha Master looked at my body and said, "You need no more protection. You have enough written on you already." I was amazed. The tattoos that were given to me by my original Buddha Master had no color and were absorbed into my body. This refugee camp Buddha Master was certainly the real deal.

I looked for ways to help others in the refugee camp. There were a lot of people that I helped so that they could prove who they were after they crossed the river. These people had lost parents, had no documentation, or were stuck in the camp for several years. I helped these people through the process of how they could go to a "third country" or, in other words, somewhere other than Laos or Thailand. I helped with United Nations translations in processing re-location paperwork for the countries that sponsored refugees, such as Australia, New Zealand, Canada, Spain, Germany, France, and Japan. The U.S. was more selective as to who it would allow into the country. For example, the U.S. would only take families with a history of being in a concentration camp or who had previously worked for the U.S., like those who worked for the CIA. The U.S. would not aid orphaned children or trafficked girls without families.

I saw what a serious problem trafficking was, so I helped locate and save young girls from this horrible criminal practice. Girls from refugee camps were easy prey for traffickers. Thai people tried to take Laotian girls out of the camps and sell them as prostitutes. I got help from a United Nations representative and human rights groups in the camp. I also used my CIA training to find out where these Thai traffickers hid the girls. Once I got the location of where the girls were being held, I took the human rights people to the city in Nakong province and reported the cases to the police. We found the girls locked up in hotels. These girls were being held prisoner in between being pimped out. When we broke into the hotels to save these girls, they would cry with relief, run out of the room and hug us. I am proud to say I worked with teams to save between 80 to 90 girls.

I worked hard at all my jobs and saved my modest earnings paid to me by the camp. I knew my residency in the camp was a temporary situation. I wanted to one day have some permanence back in my life. That included being reunited with my family. While I was not sure yet how to make that reunion possible, there was hope on the horizon that let me know it would be sooner than later.

CHAPTER TWENTY-TWO

One day in 1985, I left the refugee camp for a walk to visit a sub-station on the riverbank of the Mekong. The sub-station was made up 30 military men, many of whom I knew from my military days in Laos. Some of these men had also escaped from the concentration camps. They all were having a hard time with the communists taking over Laos. The purpose of the sub-station was to stop the communists if they tried to come across the river into Thailand. These military men also dabbled in guerilla warfare. Some of these men crossed the river back to Laos and killed communists. After they killed the communists, they brought their victims' guns back into Thailand. The Thailand government was not officially involved with this group. The government allowed these men to set up camp by the Mekong, but they were not allowed to carry their weapons outside that compound. I could not help but notice, however, that the Thai government did end up using the communists' guns.

These 30 men would also, for a price, deliver messages from refugees to their families back in Laos. These soldiers could swim well and knew how to get in and out of Laos right under the communists' noses. I could visit the sub-station because I had the necessary identification card signed by the head of the police department for the province. These military men also had another agenda. They wanted to fight and get our country back. The group kept urging me to join them. Part of me was still furious at the communists and it would be a lie to say that revenge was not on my mind. The other part of me knew that Laos was lost, that my energy was needed to reunite with my family one day and to live in peace somehow.

The future was on my mind one day when I visited the sub-station. The 30 men lived in small huts near Mekong River. Talk circled back to fighting the communists and taking Laos back from them. I told these men, "When we had a country, we had weapons supplied by the United States, we had ammunition from the United States and the communists still took over after they left us to fight for ourselves. How will your small group with your guns get Laos back? We all need to move on to the next chapter. Some of you have young children. They need to go to school. Some of you have wives. They need to have a better life. This is no life over here." I argued that the Thai government was probably using them to spy on the Lao communists. I told them, "If the Thai government one day changes like the Lao government did, you can be sure they will turn you all over to the communists and they will kill you all." This was the first time those men heard such words from someone. Their mindset was always to fight, fight, fight. I painted the political picture like it really was. We all needed to move on to a third country and start a better life for ourselves.

Not long after that meeting, those men got news out of one of the concentration camps known as Camp #5 located in Meuang Vivngsay. They delivered news to me that my father was still alive. They received this news from a former Lao military man who had once served under my father. After the war, that military man joined the communist party. While I was very happy to hear my father was alive, I was sad to learn he was not well. Apparently, my father had a stroke in 1983. It rendered him "not helpful," a classification that usually was a death sentence based on the communist way of doing things. The only one reason my father was not killed was because the military man who had once served under him knew my father was a good man. When this military man saw that my father had suffered a stroke, he felt sorry for him. He took some communist party leaders over to the concentration camp and showed them my father's condition. My father was unable to walk, had difficulty speaking and could only crawl to get around. The military man kept telling the other communist leaders of the camp that since my father has no use to them, just get some money from his family and let him go. That military man knew that bribing officers was an effective way to get people out of the camp. That was how the communists became rich because families would give up everything and anything to get their family members home.

The military man who used to work for my father was able to contact my mother in Luang Prabang. He informed my mother that her husband was in Camp #5, that he was not doing well because he suffered a stroke, and that she could pay to get him home. Without hesitation, my mother offered all her money and whatever valuables she had left to get my father back home. Camp #5 was a long distance from where my mother lived in Luang Prabang. The roads were in terrible condition, so the journey to get my father home took three or four extra days. At last, by the middle of 1985, my father arrived at the farmhouse.

After I was informed of my father's release from the concentration camp, my plan was to get him, my mother, my brother, and sister out of Laos and bring them over to Thailand. I sent a letter to my mother. I recommended to her that we wait until my father was in a little better condition to make the journey to Thailand. I also suggested we contact my other younger brother, Math, for help. Math had moved to the United States in 1979, around the time I was in the concentration camp. Math could send the money necessary to pay for the rest of the family to be smuggled over to Thailand. Thanks to Math's help, we had the 7000 baht to pay the military men on the banks of the Mekong to bring my family over.

About five or six months later, towards the end of 1985, my father was fit enough to travel again. I sent the military men from the sub-station to go pick up my family from the farmhouse. I told the three men who were going to pick up my family to be sure to gather all of their important papers and photos. Thai officials were strict about who was coming into the country, so it was important to be able to prove my father was in the military. I also instructed the military men to make sure my family brought just enough clothes to carry. Once they all reached the banks of the Mekong, all three men helped carry my father into the boat.

The trip across the river was without incident. When my family arrived in Thailand, they had to go to the immigration office and get processed. A United Nations interpreter introduced himself to help. The interpreter was immediately shocked when he saw my father because he used to be a soldier under my father's command. This man kneeled, cried, and hugged my father. He thought my father had died in the concentration camp. Once my father was recognized, no one asked any questions. They knew who he was, his papers and photo clearly showed he was high up in the military, so he was processed right away. My family was placed into a special house, separate from the rest of the refugees, until there was room in the camp.

I finally arrived at where my family was temporarily staying. When I saw my father for the first time, I was too overwhelmed with happiness to speak. My father could not speak at first, either. Our whole family was crying. We never thought we would see each other again. I must admit that I had mixed feelings seeing my father again. I was happy that he was alive, and we were able to be together again. However, my father changed a lot. It should not have been a shock given that I had also gone through severe hardships in the camp. However, my father had gone from a sharp, handsome, fearless, and powerful general to a white haired and weakened old man. He was paralyzed on his right side, his speech was slurred, and he was scared to talk about the communists. At first, when I tried to talk to him about what the communists had done, he would say, "Do not say anything about them or they will put us in jail or kill us."

My father and I instead talked and cried about other things during that first day of being reunited. Despite all of his skills and experience, my father had serious doubts about whether he could survive in the concentration camp. My father used the same strategy that I did. He never told the communists the truth. Even though they knew who my father was, he never admitted to it. He told me the communists beat him up often. He passed out many times from the beatings. They interrogated him, he lied to them, then he would get beat up until he passed out. They forced my father to do hard labor. They tried to trick him by with same lie they always used: "If you tell us the truth, you will go home." The prisoners who broke down and told the truth were then tied to a jeep and dragged around the camp until they died. Most of the 40 generals who were brought in as prisoners in the camp were killed.

My father told me that Uncle Ouane was also prisoner in Camp #5. It was there that Uncle Ouane admitted to my father that I did the right thing to arrest him. He also admitted that he initially ordered his men to shoot me when I approached his house. What caused Uncle Ouane to retract his order at the last moment was that he saw a vision of my late grandfather's face. My father also told me that Uncle Ouane was killed in the concentration camp. The communists tied him up to a jeep and drove/dragged him around the camp until he died.

My father and I spoke about how my half-brother Thao Yai treated me when I sought help from him after my first escape. My father was not surprised by his other son's behavior. He knew that Thao Yai had his mother's personality and that he was jealous of me from a young age. He admitted that Thao Yai was just a bad person. He assured me that I did not need to ever talk to him again.

We wondered if there had not been a disconnect with my grandfather's family in Japan after he died in 1965 if they would have helped our family somehow after Laos fell to the communists. Our talks then turned to the political situation in Laos. My father's initial fear to discuss it had worn off. During his time in the concentration camp, my father felt betrayed by the CIA and the U.S. military. He had many questions about why things turned out the way they did. The Lao military vowed to would fight until the end so why was it that the U.S. stopped its support? My father wanted to someday talk to people in the U.S. who were responsible for its involvement in the war and get some answers. My father thought about how he once had everything: family, money, houses, and cars. The next thing he knows he is a prisoner in a concentration camp, first being beaten within his life, then crawling around because he suffered a stroke. He felt that he had nothing. My father and I had the same thoughts while we were both prisoners in different camps. While we were together again, those thoughts still haunted us both.

CHAPTER TWENTY-THREE

The U.S. dropped more than two million tons of bombs on Laos during 580,000 bombing missions. It was equal to a planeload of bombs every 8 minutes, 24 hours a day for 9 years straight. Laos was the most heavily bombed country in history. They were part of the U.S. Secret War in Laos to support our Royal Lao Government against the communist Pathet Lao. The bombings destroyed many villages and displaced hundreds of thousands of Lao civilians during the nine-year war. When the U.S. withdrew from Laos, hundreds of thousands of refugees fled the country. Many of them resettled in the United States.

As a result of this Secret War, it was not a secret that we Laotians were disappointed with the U.S. government for leaving Laos in the middle of a war-torn mess. The U.S. wiped its' hands of us and told us to swim or drown. We thought they should have stayed and help fight the communists until the end. My father believed that there were things we did not, and would never, know about the U.S. agenda in Laos. While I was assisting the United Nations representatives in the refugee camp, one man I worked with was named John Tucker. Tucker was my boss in the refugee camp, and we would have conversations about the aftermath in Laos. Tucker explained to me that he believed one reason the U.S. stopped supporting the Lao government during the war had to do with domestic political changes and pressures. The anti-war protests and Nixon's involvement with Watergate most likely forced the U.S. to take care of itself first.

Tucker's explanation at least gave my father and me some context. Tucker went on to say that despite what we may have thought about the U.S., it was still the most desirable country in the world to live. There were freedoms and opportunities that we could not enjoy anywhere else. While there were a lot of rules to relocate to the U.S., things could be expedited for my family because my father and I had worked for the CIA. I thought about this possibility of moving to the U.S. One of my younger brothers, Math, was already living there. I thought about the guerilla group camped out by the Mekong River who still wanted to fight to win our country back. That small group clearly had no chance. Besides, now that my family was reunited, I could not leave them again to fight another war that could not be won. I had a wife and son in Laos, but I could not return to them in

263

this climate. There was no future for me in Thailand. That country would not be allowing refugees to stay there forever. The only way for me to have any kind of a life and a future was to relocate to another country.

I spoke to Tucker and others from the United Nations more about what life would be like in the U.S. It would be different, from the food to the customs. It would not be easy, but I had certainly survived harsher conditions than culture shock. I still had conflicting feelings about the U.S because it had left Laos vulnerable for the eventual communist take-over. The benefits outweighed any burdens of starting a new life in the U.S.

My family and I boarded a bus and left the refugee camp in Thailand in the summer of 1985 or 1986. From the refugee camp, we traveled to Bangkok, stayed there for a few days then boarded a 747-airplane bound for the Philippines. For the next six months, we stayed in a transitional refugee camp like the one in Thailand. Once again, I worked as an interpreter for them. The camp provided information and training about what to expect when refugees arrived in the U.S. They helped us with our English and gave us advice and tips about how to navigate the new customs and culture. Not only did I learn these things, but I helped interpret the information for other refugees. Our stay in the Philippines was uneventful, expect that my younger brother and sister were sick with malaria.

When we boarded the plane to travel to America, my mind raced with thoughts. I thought that because of my previous escapes that someone would follow me, hunt me down and kill me. I wanted to believe that because I was going to the land of freedom, nobody would hurt me anymore. Of course, that would be naïve, after everything I had been through. I thought about my family back in Laos. I choked up thinking about my son. He was so young when I fled Luang Prabang that I feared he would never know me. I prayed that in the future, if all was well and politics allowed it, I would go back to Laos to see my wife and son again. Until then, I had to face the unknown and the future in a new country. I had a feeling, though, that I would be OK. I had faced the unknown many times before and had survived.

EPILOGUE

The following parable was mentioned to me: "Gold will always be gold. You can throw it in the dirt, in a pit, anywhere, and at the end when you wash it up, it will always be yellow gold." No matter what had happened to me - being held prisoner in a concentration camp, losing my country because of war, enduring a broken family, torture and bloodshed, witnessing the killing of other like animals and doing the killing myself – I was still a good person. I did good deeds and I cared for others whenever I could. I believe that if you do good, good will return to you in the end.

My story is real. The atrocities I witnessed are real. My passion to protect my country and my family from communism was, and continues to be, real. While the war in Laos may have ended long ago, there are people in the world today who deny the existence of the concentration camps, of the torture and of the murders of those who did not believe in communism. There are also people who refuse to discuss what really happened. They fear that if they go against the communists they will be killed. Today, nobody in Laos will go to the areas where the concentration camps were located. If they attempted to do so, they would be on the blacklist of the current Lao government. They would also not be allowed to return to Laos. Only when the government changes for the better will there be more transparency about the past.

Today, there are many communists out there who know about me. They are trying to discredit me and call me a liar. The communists want the world and history to believe their "truth." They believe that anyone who says anything contrary to their truth should be disbelieved and punished. They are fearful of the world and history learning the facts of what really happened. For them to ever acknowledge what they did in Laos and the existence of the concentration camps would expose them for who they truly are.

I do not know for certain how many survivors from the camps there are. Most prisoners who escaped or were released were not in good health. There could be 10 to 15 survivors from my camp. After I arrived in the U.S., I found out there was a survivor there from the group that escaped from the camp near the airport the Russians were building. This man had split from the group, had run day and night, ended up in Vientiane and then crossed over to Thailand.

The CIA supposedly had no idea prior to 1975 that there was a plan for concentration camps. No camps were set up by the Lao communists themselves. The way it worked was that they used the prisoners to set up their own camp while dressed in their own full green colored uniforms. That clever ploy made it appear like we were building our own camp. Only years later, after an escapee from Laos made it to the Thailand refugee camp, were the details of the existence of the camps given to the CIA. Just as the U.S. engaged in a secret war in Laos, the eventual occupants of our country kept the concentration camps a secret from the world.

Even after my father arrived in the U.S., he could not find peace. He always repeated that he had confidence and 100% trust in the CIA and U.S. military during the war. After the war, while he was a prisoner in the concentration camp, my father felt betrayed by our allies. He also was depressed. He felt he had failed his country and his troops. So many of his men, his brother and one of his sons were killed during the war. Once he lived in the U.S., he tried to understand what happened. He concluded that the geopolitics had changed and shifted, and Laos suffered because of it. He also felt he had no support to bring up these issues when he came to the U.S. He once said to me before he passed away, "Nothing is certain. Remember how it used to be and what we used to have? We were on top of the world and now we have nothing." At that time, we were begging the U.S. for help and living on food stamps to survive. My father lost the will to fight for anything anymore. As a result, he never got the answers he sought about why the U.S. treated Laos the way it did. As for myself, I will never forgive the communists for what they did to me, my family, my people, and my country. As for the CIA, now I have a better understanding about the political issues that were at play, so I forgave the U.S. for pulling out of Laos.

My original Buddha Master passed away in 1972. I did not attend the funeral because I was on the front lines fighting. However, his presence has never left me. One time during the war, I was on patrol with my platoon. As I was walking, I felt something in my body that warned me to be more careful than usual. That, I believe, was the presence of my Buddha Master. Sometimes he would come to me in a dream. I was in a near-fatal accident in 2008. The truck I was driving in flipped over down an embankment. I saw my Master while I was unconscious, and he said he was going to stay with me for a while.

When I came to, I was able to punch out the windshield to escape and I survived the accident. Just a few months ago, when I left home to go to work, something was moving in my body in the morning, as if warning me to be very careful. After work, I realized that two men were following me. I was ready to defend myself. While I have no scientific proof of this, I do believe that my sixth sense of danger is attributed to my Buddha Master. My second Buddha Master ended up escaping to Thailand, but he unfortunately died in the refugee camp.

After being forced to labor in the fields by the Lao communists, the King and Queen of Laos died in their concentration camp. A dynasty that had endured for 600 years was snuffed out just like that.

In 1977, the U.S. officially recognized the valor of the Hmong guerilla fighters. A small stone with a copper plaque was placed to represent the honor of the Hmong fighters in Arlington National Cemetery. However, the plaque cannot fully resolve the soldiers' plight in Southeast Asia. Veterans and refugees like myself are worried that the communist rulers of our homeland still have a significant grudge against us.

It is estimated that more than 360,000 Laotians who survived the atrocities of war and the Lao communist regime, about 10 percent of the population, fled the country between1975 and 1992. There was good reason for that escape. Communist efforts to establish collective work groups and village-wide agricultural cooperatives and bring education and bureaucracy to rural areas were futile in terms of improving the standard of living. Also, the communist government, while it did not abolish Buddhist religious life, tried to control it which led to a decrease in the number of monks. Overall, repression and "re-education" changed my homeland for the worse.

My life in the U.S. has had its up and downs. I re-married and had four more children. I was a single father for a long time after I broke up with my ex-wife. For years, I was a truck driver. I worked hard and made good money. After being involved in that terrible trucking accident in 2008, I suffered from a broken back. I had also grown weary of being away from home so much and I wanted to do something that truly helped others. Two years after my trucking accident, I started a new business, one which I believe would have made my grandfather proud. I am the owner of a residential board and care home for the elderly and the disabled. With my background, I was well suited for this new career change.

I could easily handle the basic medical tasks that were required for my patients – dressing wounds, giving shots, and managing medicines. I was also able to relate to my patients based on the lessons I learned from my grandfather and from leading soldiers on the battlefield. In fact, it turns out that the most difficult patients and disagreeable patients are regularly referred to my board and care facility because I have earned a reputation for taking good care of them. A social worker from the county once said, "If this house is not able to care for a patient, no one can." Just like my grandfather was always on call for his patients and just as I made sure I took care of my soldiers first; I make sure my patients are taken care of before I do anything for myself. When my wife packs me a lunch, I end up sharing it with my patients if they have not yet been served their meal. I have been able to earn the trust and respect of my patients. They know I always listen to them and care about their well-being, so they end up listening to me when the time comes. When I think about it now, my whole life has made it possible for me to successfully care for these patients who I consider a part of my family.

I am also involved in the Joint Military Assistance Command (JMAC). JMAC is nonprofit organization dedicated to helping needy and retired veterans from all branches and their families. JMAC offers mental health counseling, disability assistance, benefits assistance, and food banks. I am a Major General in this organization. I help train a diverse volunteer corps and I have also helped veterans who have come home and are dealing with post-traumatic stress. We also provide military units for funeral services for any fallen U.S. soldiers. We even provided the full military service for General Vang Pao who moved to the U.S. after the war and died in 2011.

I went back to Laos in 2007. I tried to track down the police captain named Aumpai who helped me once I arrived in Thailand. I could not find him, but I was told he was a general and lived in Bangkok. I reunited with Colonel Phet who had been so helpful to me. He happened to be married to a cousin of mine. Colonel Phet was living in a small house. He was happy to see me, but he was upset that he did not have any food for me. I told him, "Don't worry about me. I will buy you food." I went to the market and bought the family food. I saw that Colonel Phet's house needed some repairs, so I helped fix things and paid for other repairs. Colonel Phet's children could not go to school, and he could not afford their books and tuition. I offered to pay for school for them for a full year.

Colonel Phet was very grateful, but I reminded him that he had saved my life, so I was the one who wanted to show my gratitude. Colonel Phet told me that the communists lied to everyone. They had told him when Laos was finally under communist control, they would give him everything, the big house and a lot of money. When Colonel Phet asked them to give him a big house, the communist leaders said, "We are not going to give you anything. If we give it to you then we must give it to everybody who asks. We don't have enough money so you must take care of yourself." Colonel Phet was so mad that he was tricked by the communist's lies. During my visit I also gave my cousin some money to start a little grocery store to take care of her children. I wanted to pay back the people who helped me. I also saw that the tank that was blown up by the NVA that killed my brother was still in Laos as a memorial to the war.

I went to visit Laos again in 2011. Along with my now-grown son who I had left behind in 1984, I visited my half-brother, Thao Yai. I told Thao Yai, "You have the property that belonged to our grandfather. I am asking you to share some of the property with your nephew, my son." Still the jealous and greedy person he always was, Thao Yai sneered at us and said, "I do not give away anything. You are in the United States now. All of this belongs to me. You want to sue me, go ahead. Nobody has money like me in this town." I was upset with Thao Yai's reaction. I tried to talk to him a couple more times, but Thao Yai continued to be hostile towards me and could not be reasoned with. I reminded him that the law in Laos was if a husband and wife got divorced because the wife committed the adultery, the property would not go to the wife's children and would instead go to the husband. The facts were clear that Thao Yai legally had no right to the property; our father divorced Thao Yai's mother because she had committed adultery.

My oldest son brought legal action against Thao Yai in 2011. In 2012, my son learned that Thao Yai's wife hired someone to kill him. My son had to hire bodyguards. He also wore body armor and carried a gun. Two or three weeks later, my son was at the bank. A hit man fired at my son, but he missed. A second attempt on my son's life happened, when he and his bodyguards were at a restaurant It was very busy, and the restaurant was near the market. This time, two hit men tried to shoot my son. My son used to be in the military, so he was able to escape. His bodyguards exchanged shots with the hit men. They caught one hit man, then later caught the other one. Police connected them to Thao Yai's wife. During this time, Thao Yai suffered a major stroke. Thao Yai's wife was thrown in prison. Karma indeed came back to get Thao Yai and his wife. My grandfather's property now belongs to my son. Thao Yai is still alive today, but he is paralyzed and has a feeding tube. As difficult as it was to do, I have finally been able to forgive Thao Yai for every horrible thing he did to me and my family.

I have seen and experienced what selfishness and greed have done to make people and countries act in unimaginable ways. I have tried my best to live by the Five Precepts and treat others as I would want to be treated. Of course, one does not need to be a Buddhist to live a good life and treat others humanely. One does not even have to have any religious beliefs to do those things. If only everyone could try to just be good, thoughtful of others and treat everyone equally, the world would certainly be a better place.

I have never forgotten where I came from. It is true I was born into great privilege. My father taught me that I had to be my own man, make my own life, work hard for what I want, be a good person and do the right thing. Nothing was ever handed to me when I was growing up, even though my father could afford to give me what I wanted. The best thing my father ever gave me was how to build good character, work ethic and how to gain people's trust and confidence in me. It was a priceless gift that served me well and helped me to survive when everything was taken from me.

As a result of my experiences, I have a hard time trusting people who have left Laos and come to the U.S. I never know if these people still have some remaining loyalty to the communist government there and want to discredit the truth of what happened during and after the war. Having lived in America for many years now, I trust the government of this country more now. I never have, and never will, trust the communist government in Laos. Nothing has improved in my home country; it seems like it has only gotten worse and more corrupt.

The one thing I would change in my life would be during the time right before I left to go the "seminar" to supposedly learn about the ways of how the communists were going to work with us in Laos. Despite my misgivings about it, I agreed to go. There was a Lao communist man there who took me aside and told me, "Your job is really difficult, so I need you to stay here and help me. Let the others go." I thought since we were told that the training would only take two months, that I would be back soon enough to help this man. Looking back on it now, I believe this man was giving me a hint that there was nothing good waiting for me at this "seminar." If I could turn the clock back, I would have listened to this man and stayed. I would also have taken the CIA's offer to come to the U.S. when I had the chance.

The communists never figured out that I had used a fake name in the concentration camp or when I returned to Laos after my escape. While I could have returned to using my birth name when I arrived in the U.S., I decided to go by "Kevin" because it would be easier for everyone. My very close friends call me "Mr. Lion," a nickname given to me because they all think I'm a sleeping lion: quiet when I need to be but ready to roar when necessary.

Official Support Letter from General Dean Murphy

ABOUT THE AUTHORS

Captain Sounthone Ratanakone

Captain Ratanakone was born into a privileged life, the son of a general in the Royal Lao Army and grandson of a prestigious doctor. He was educated in Laos and later earned his law degree. He served honorably in the Royal Lao Army, was a decorated war hero, a CIA operative in the Secret War in Laos during the Vietnam War, and a POW in a communist concentration camp.

Captain Ratanakone has lived his life with the great principles and values he learned from his family and from his Buddhist religion. He has always striven to have a clear mind, body, and soul and to follow the Five Precepts.

Todd Samovitz

Todd Samovitz pivoted from the practice of law and became an accomplished writer in film, television and comics as well as the author or ghost author of 25 books. He is a graduate of the University of Michigan and Southwestern University School of Law. Samovitz lives in Southern California with his wife and three children.

CPSIA information can be obtained
at www.ICGtesting.com
Printed in the USA
BVHW071245311022
650744BV00002B/64